Memories
of
High Wycombe

Part of the
Memories
series

*The Publishers would like to thank the following companies for supporting
the production of this book*

Main Sponsor

IL Beeks (HW) Limited

William Bartlett

Buckinghamshire Housing Association

Ercol Furniture Limited

High Wycombe Central Aid Society

Isaac Lord Limited

Pipers Corner School

Southern Counties Saw Company Limited

First published in Great Britain by True North Books Limited
Units 3 - 5 Heathfield Industrial Park
Elland West Yorkshire
HX5 9AE
Tel. 01422 377977
© Copyright: True North Books Limited 1999

ISBN 1 900463 84 9

Text, design and origination by True North Books Limited
Printed and bound by The Amadeus Press Limited

Memories are made of this

Memories. We all have them: people, places and events, some good and some bad. Our memories of the place where we grew up are usually tucked away in a very special place in our mind. The best are probably connected with our childhood and youth, when we longed to be grown up and paid no attention to adults who told us to enjoy being young, as these were the best years of our lives. We look back now and realise that they were right.

Old photographs bring our memories flooding back - coronations and celebrations; talking pictures, Technicolor and television; the war years, rationing, and the shared hopes and fears which created such a warm community spirit; buying things made of nylon and plastic; fashions which took trouser-bottoms and hemlines from drainpipes and mini-

skirts to the other extreme; Doris Day, Acker Bilk, Elvis Presley and the Beatles; the jitterbug, the tango and discos; Ford Populars and Minis; decimalisation. Life changed so much over the years. Some changes were big, some small; some altered our lives in ways we never anticipated. Who in the early days of motoring could have foreseen the motorways and traffic systems of the latter decades of the 20th century? Did any of us realise, when we first saw a computer, what a tremendous impact they would have on our lives? Self-service supermarkets and frozen food made our lives easier - but at the expense of our friendly little corner shops. Nostalgia is always such a mixture of feelings . . . We hope that the collection of pictures in this book will remind you of happy days in bygone eras - and who knows, you might even have been there when one of the photographs was taken!

Contents

Events & occasions

The celebrations in High Wycombe in 1937 in honour of the Coronation of King George VI were ones of joy and relief. The joy was obvious. We had a new King. The relief was equally obvious. This was a time for the people of this country to put behind them the memories of the three hundred and twenty-five day reign of George's elder brother, Edward VIII. In the previous year their father, George V, had died. Edward succeeded him only to abdicate rather give up his association with an American divorcee, Mrs Simpson. It is hard to imagine today such a situation causing such grief and turmoil as it did then. But there was distress, and Edward's 'final and irrevocable decision' for the sake of a woman he loved had all the hallmarks of a second-rate Hollywood movie - except it was real and was important to this country and to the Empire. So a shy retiring man was thrust on to the throne. The relief was obvious and the celebrations heartfelt.

Above: After the day's parade there was what was later described as a 'colourful and glittering spectacle' in the Town Hall as over five hundred people gathered for the masked carnival ball. It was said also that the ball lasted until 'Wycombe's milkmen were setting out on their morning rounds'. Costumes varied from the Mayor's Elizabethan attire to Roman soldiers, John Bull, naturally, and the headmaster of the Royal Grammar School, some may say appropriately, as Julius Caesar. One report commented that some of the young girls were in dresses that 'started before they had begun'. 'Fashion' was the rage then. Nylons had been introduced into the country in the late 30s and being daring was a compulsion for some. In fact there was a 'most daring' prize at the ball won by a young lady dressed as a sunbather. The 'most daring' man was Cupid. Earlier that evening there had been a fireworks display. A programme of dancing in the High Street to music provided by the High Wycombe Town Military Band had been planned. However the crowds were found more in doorways sheltering from the rain than thronging the street with merriment. There were, however, some daring and enterprising souls who commandeered a radiogram and, despite the rain, danced to its music after the band had cried off. Certainly many in High Wycombe had entered into the spirit of the occasion and that mood was reflected throughout the town.

Right: The Carnival was the highlight of the town's celebrations with individuals and groups encouraged to take part, parading through the crowded streets of the town. The decorated streets and shops and businesses added to the colourful spectacle and there was a patriotic fervour which would serve the country well in the following dark years. The holiday atmosphere had certainly encouraged the crowds to line the streets and seek good vantage points for the Carnival parade, led by the Carnival Queen and her retinue. It followed the traditional route from the Rye through the town's main streets to the Guildhall. There were other events too prior to the day. The Mayor had visited some of the town's schools. The visit followed an established pattern. The Mayor would be introduced; he would talk about the Royal Family and the Coronation; the National Anthem and other patriotic songs were sung and finally there would be three cheers for the Mayor and Their Majesties. Members of the council presented to each child a souvenir spoon, the top of which bore the head of the King and Queen and the date of the Coronation. A memento worth keeping. There will still be some hidden away in a drawer or treasure box!

Above: High Wycombe was transformed for the Coronation again into a resemblance of Venice at carnival time. Beneath festoons, garlands and flags the pavements were crowded with visitors and local people. The entrances to the town at Pann Mill and at Oxford Street were marked with decorative archways of bunting topped by huge golden crowns suspended under the Union flag. High Street and Church Street were transformed. The shops and business premises had also responded to the call. The Library, the Post Office, the Town Hall and Municipal Offices were decorated with shrubs, window boxes and flags while floodlighting of these buildings and of the Guildhall gave them an even more striking effect. One outstanding display was to be seen outside High Wycombe Technical Institute. It was made by the boys themselves and showed that their technical ingenuity was not confined to the classroom. It appeared again that the town, as it had done two years earlier for the new king's father's Silver Jubilee, was prepared to ensure that it could and should celebrate national royal occasions with something other than the ordinary. For the circumstances leading to this Coronation were themselves other than ordinary and totally unexpected.

Right: White Hart Street was the first street to be decorated as a whole, although there are not many spectators in this photograph to admire it. They do seem intent on celebrating for all their worth. The street did not come under the scheme of municipal decorations but all twenty-seven traders combined and produced this effective result. The whole street from Paul's Row to Queen Square was covered in red, white and blue. Frogmoor pavement island was surrounded by Venetian poles supporting coloured lights while the shops carried their own forms of decoration. All streets were similarly decorated; Union Jacks and flags of the Empire were everywhere. A local newspaper report commented that there were enough signalling flags 'to have caused an international incident if displayed in the proper combination at sea'. Shops reflected the glamour of the actual Coronation procession with models of the State Coach, richly coloured in gold, in many windows. It was not possible to enter any street in the town without seeing that patriotism, coupled with civic pride, was very much alive in all parts of the town. Photographs of the King, his Queen, Elizabeth, and their two daughters, Princess Elizabeth and Princess Margaret Rose, abounded. The memories of the year the country had three kings were behind the people now. It was a time to celebrate and look forward.

Crowds gather in High Street on this damp Thursday in June 1911 to celebrate the Coronation of King George V who had acceded to the throne the previous year. The celebrations spread into the next day and over the weekend. They varied from the formal service in the parish church to the highly organised carnival on a very wet Friday and to a masked fancy dress ball in the Town Hall. A fireworks display and a bonfire were held. At a civic old folks' party the men were presented with a pipe and tobacco and the ladies snuff and for those who did not imbibe they were given sweets. The town's streets were colourfully decorated, especially High Street, scene of this Children's Procession. The children had been identified through their Sunday Schools. Each was given a souvenir medal which they wore as they proceeded from their schools to the High Street, each school identified by a placard. The 'Unattached' must have had some significance with Sunday Schools. Six thousand children and thousands of adults met here as close as they could to the Red Lion for the singing of the National Anthem. The procession then left for Daws Hill Park. The thick drizzle did not mar the festivities which took place in the park before the children returned to their Sunday Schools for tea. High Wycombe had welcomed the new King and his Queen, Mary, with enthusiasm despite the fact they knew very little about either of them except they were the King and Queen of this country. That is all that mattered.

Above: King George V, known affectionately as the 'Sailor King', celebrated his Silver Jubilee with Queen Mary in May 1935. He was reputed to be behind the idea that 'Abide With Me' should be sung at the FA Cup Final. He was said to be a stuffy rather dull man but he did endear himself to British people. Therefore this occasion was celebrated by High Wycombe with all the enthusiasm it could muster. The corporation sent official greetings; streets, shops and offices were decorated with flags and bunting. Flowers were especially planted. Civic buildings were floodlit and some public houses installed neon lights. On the day of the Jubilee the sun shone brightly. The bells of the Parish Church, like an alarm clock of anticipation, sounded out first thing their messages of joy. A civic service of thanksgiving was held in the church in the morning with the sermon preached by the Bishop of Oxford. In the early afternoon the crowds began to gather on the High Street for one of the highlights of the festivities. The town's Military Band played the National Anthem which was sung by the people with a patriotic gusto. Then came the highlight of this part of the celebrations - a massed choir of one thousand, five hundred schoolchildren, conducted by Mr E E Soons, Headmaster of Green Street School, singing outside the Red Lion. One must wonder where and how they could have rehearsed for this. Rehearse they must because their renditions of 'God Bless Our Native Land' and 'O England' were enthusiastically received by the large crowd for which the children themselves were noisily grateful.

Above right: After the singing it was time for the traditional Carnival procession. It is interesting that on every grand occasion in the first half of the twentieth century carnivals were the order

of the day when a town wanted to celebrate. Yet since possibly the Coronation in 1953 there does not seem to have been that fervour. The High Wycombe Carnival of 1935 was a great sight, likened to the famous Carnival in Venice for its merriment. The procession of one hundred and sixty decorated cycles, motor cars, lorries and motor coaches led by the Mayor began its journey in Green Street The crowds all along the route to the High Street had to be kept back by marshals on horseback dressed as cowboys. It was a brilliant scene as the parade entered High Street with the colours of the decorations, the floats and the bandsmen mingling together. The carnival floats were full of ingenuity and humour with entries having been received from businesses, shops and factories, children's societies and clubs, municipal organisations, in fact all aspects of the town's life were represented. And towering above everything seated on a lorry, decorated naturally in red, white and blue, was Britannia keeping a cool head despite the heat of the day, her costume and the excitement all around her.

The Mayoress of High Wycombe, Mrs G H Brocklehurst, crowns the Carnival Queen, Edith Powell. This proved to be a day to remember for the Carnival Queen. She had led the carnival parade in a green carriage with her maids of honour dressed in pink and pages in blue. It would be interesting today if any of those maids and pages and maybe the Queen Edith herself can recall that day in May 1935. What followed after the parade left High Street was remarkable for events in those days. The procession set off for the Rye and so did the crowd, estimated to be fifteen thousand, eager to catch a glimpse of High Wycombe's own Coronation. Fortunately good order and good humour prevailed and most of the crowd were afforded a good view of her 'throne'. A fanfare of trumpets heralded Queen Edith's crowning by the Mayoress and the ceremony took place smoothly and with all the pomp and dignity appropriate to the occasion. There followed a display of folk dancing, of physical exercises and more dancing by pupils of Miss Hilda Bailey. Then, to the delight of all, Queen Edith's departure from the Rye was rather different from the way she arrived. She sailed along the Dyke on her gondola. Echoes of Venice again!

Below: Lord Lincolnshire's funeral - and a note from his widow to the Mayor read 'Daws Hill, High Wycombe 13th June 1928. To His Worship the Mayor of Wycombe - Dear Mr Stacey - I am sending this note to tell you the sad news that my beloved husband died this morning of heart failure. He spoke so much of Wycombe and his love for the people - and it made him very happy at the last to know that the Wendover Way scheme which he had so much at heart was completed in his lifetime.......Lady Lincolnshire.' Lord Lincolnshire was a true friend of the town and did indeed have the town's interests at heart. He was a landowner and during his life was highly regarded by everyone who had dealings with him rich and poor, young and old alike. He was described as a man of Wycombe and of the people who lived there. In his lifetime he had been a Cabinet Minister, Colonial Governor, Member of London County Council and all the time a friend of the town. And so it should be that as well the Memorial Service in St Margaret's, Westminster, there should be his funeral in the town of High Wycombe. There were many tributes from political, sporting and religious sources. In this modern age where there is a certain amount of cynicism expressed about the motives and actions of politicians and people in public life, it is worth recalling that there were, and obviously still are, people at all levels who do wish to serve the community.

Right: So the people of High Wycombe turned out in their thousands to pay their last respects to a man of the town. An hour before the funeral procession there were knots of people gathering in the High Street. At 11.30am the black coated procession from the Town Hall to the Parish Church began, followed by a contingent of Royal Horse Guards. The cortege left the family home and drove to the church. By now the crowds were vast and a thin cordon of police had great difficulty holding the line in front of the War Memorial. The street was lined with people; faces peered from every upper window; viewpoints included window-sills and roofs of cars. The coffin was led into church by Lord Carrington, his brother. The crowds remained in their place during the service. Afterwards they watched in respectful silence as the cortege left the church bound for the interment in the Moulsoe Churchyard. Again there were large crowds made up of people long associated with the dead peer. Proper and due respect had been paid to a man who had served his country and town with such dedication.

Above: Great rejoicing throughout the town and county as the local soldiers return home at the end of the Boer War in 1902. A decorated arch was erected at the top of Crendon Street close to the Railway Station for the men of the Bucks Militia to march through. High Wycombe was the reception centre for these troops as well as having a Military Hospital in Benjamin Road. A large crowd had gathered at High Wycombe Railway Station including the Mayor and Corporation and relatives of returning volunteers. A distant whistle heralded the approach of the train and the decorated engine glided into the station. Three cheers were raised for the 'soldiers' wives and sweethearts' but before the volunteers could disembark, they had to wait for the arrival of an ordinary passenger train on the up line. Eventually the Buckinghamshire men were given a rousing welcome and the procession of the Constabulary, the Fire Brigade and then the 'khaki clad heroes of the day' soon formed for the march to the Parish Church. As they emerged from the station yard, the band played 'Soldiers of the King' and there was a tremendous roar from the crowd. The procession then set off towards Crendon Street, rather too quickly for the liking of the civic dignitaries who were soon cut off from the main body and submerged by the enthusiastic crowd. The narrowness of Crendon Street did not help and confusion reigned, resulting in a mass of civilians, the civic and the military forming one vast surge of people. It all added to the atmosphere and all that mattered was the volunteers were home.

Above right: By the time the procession reached the more spacious High Street the 'symmetry of the procession was somewhat restored' and the progress to the Parish Church was more orderly and according to the arranged programme. The principal street of the town was magnificently decorated and the crowds so immense they left only a narrow space in the centre for the procession. Every inch of standing room was taken and every window and balcony crowded. The local newspaper remarked on the colourful sight of the ladies in their dresses while handkerchiefs being waved seemed to be the welcoming order of the day. Comparing this with the stain-worn khaki of the men who had recently fought in Africa, the contrast could not have been more vivid. As the procession passed down the street, the cheering rang out on all sides and it was remarked that it was difficult to hear the military music. The crowds were equally as large and enthusiastic in Church Square as the procession entered past a guard of honour through the South Porch of the 'Cathedral of Bucks' with great solemnity and dignity . The people of High Wycombe had given an appropriate welcome home to its soldiers.

Below: Frogmoor was the town's version of Hyde Park Corner, where political speakers espousing ideas of Utopia or perceived views of someone else's hell, holders of all religious beliefs and anyone else with a message or dire warning attracted attention. Here we can witness the power of advertising and this elephant certainly attracted attention - so did the photographer. Those young children in their Eton Collars and boaters appear fascinated by all that is happening. We may assume it is an Indian elephant promoting tea from India or is that too subtle and it is just a novelty? Whatever, the name of Salmon's tea floats gently in the air and no doubt the organisers are well on the way to believing what we now hold to be part of our lives -

it pays to advertise. Tea was, however, still considered to be luxury until about 1930. County Tea was to become Gardner's Wine and Spirits while on the other side of Bull Lane Peace Jones were rather entrepreneural with their provisions, china and tailoring departments. A fascinating photograph indeed!

Bottom: The imposing frontages of the High Street shops and businesses and naturally of the Red Lion and in the rear the Parish Church provide an imposing backdrop to the activities taking place in the street itself. The sunshine helps to make this 1930 band contest such a grand sight. The colour of the uniforms, the gleam of the instruments, the shop blinds and the crowd of people enjoying the warmth and the procession make High Street once again a most fitting setting for the event. There are streets which lend themselves to processions like this. High Street in 1950 is one. The long line of road, the width that is offered, the grandness of the surrounds make this a wonderful sight. And to make it all so much more interesting look at the stately policeman at the junction with Corporation Street. Look at the equally stately cars and even the lone cyclist does not look to be out of place. Finally look at the little boy proudly heading the band. He will have had a wonderful day, something for him and the bands and the crowd to remember. A photograph of grand High Wycombe.

Like all major thoroughfares in any town or city High Street was the centre of any parade and procession. Whether they were processions, parades or carnivals, it was the constant focal point. What makes this photograph all the more interesting is the combi-

nation of various elements in it. There is the street itself looking away from the Guildhall; there are the market stalls and the occasional shopper; there is the crowd of people more interested in the military parade than shopping and obviously more of that

parade to come. But what about that open-topped bus? Is it on parade too? Doubtful if those passengers are just getting on. More likely it is an intrusion into the main event. But it does give us a chance to view a relic of the past. Towns and cities needed a more flexible transport system to cater for the growth of out of town estates. Here it is in a photograph which contains so many features of life, including the fashions of the people in it, in High Wycombe in the 1920s.

Right: For most of the nineteenth century this country had no ambulance service and it was only in the 1870s that a great 'ambulance movement' began. Leading this original movement was the St John Ambulance Association founded in 1877. It had become familiar with ambulance design in the wars of that period and coined the term 'first aid' from a combination of first treatment and the society's nickname 'National Aid'. From small beginnings grew the service with which we are familiar today. It was a slow growth, confined in the beginning to industrial areas. The service produced ambulance textbooks, awarded certificates and trained workers. It also trained the police and fire service and in fact some of the early ambulance services were run by the police or the fire brigade. Odd though it may seem it took a long while for this innovation to be accepted. The brigades were often tainted with the cries of 'bodysnatchers' in the early days. The service was for many years entirely voluntary and relied on charity and funding to continue. This new ambulance in High Wycombe in 1934 would not be as a result of local authority funding. Money for it would have come from a different source. Local Authorities were not bound to provide ambulance services until 1974. Before that they could hire St John Ambulance or the Red Cross. This new ambulance is a beginning but it did take a long time for the service to be properly trained and equipped.

Below: 'Old Bill' the famous wartime bus was brought out of retirement for the funeral procession of London Transport bus driver Frank Wright of Desborough Avenue on 1st February 1938. This solemn cortege has all the appearance of a state funeral as it approaches the Parish Church and it is pretty certain that it would not happen today. There appears here a sense of belonging to the service, identifying with it. There was a pride in delivering an efficient transport system; it was a point of honour no matter whether you were a uniformed conductor or driver or a suited manager or an overalled mechanic. Some drivers did like to think they were the 'kings' however. This communal feeling had lasted for many years and continued to do so for some years afterwards. So a funeral turn out for this gentleman was out of respect for a working colleague. That sense of identity is not so prevalent these days. Who provides the bus service now is a more modern concern. The funeral procession here highlights a different emphasis.

launch took place without a hitch. Someone did remark at the time, however, about the dilemma mariners off the coast of Southend faced that weekend should they get into trouble.

Top: A team line-up in July 1917 of men and mostly young girls at this factory in London Road making ammunition boxes for the war effort. They all seem quite content and in some cases happy but don't they look young? That is until we recall that the education system was not as sophisticated as it is today and these girls would have left school at fourteen or earlier, if they went at all. With so many men at the front line in the 'War to end all Wars' the government needed workers for munitions factories, transport and office jobs. The only choice, strange as it may sound today, was to employ women. For the first time a British Government was involved in the planning and running of industry. Most of the women came from domestic service or other poorly paid work or no work at all. There was a special arrangement with trade unions which meant that women could replace skilled men for wartime work only. On the whole the women worked in poor conditions but they would have been better paid than before. If the war did nothing else, it gave them a chance to work alongside men or even replace them in clerical jobs at least. After all this was a real step forward - they were not allowed to vote yet.

Above: The Lifeboat had been brought to land-locked High Wycombe from Southend-on-Sea and proved to be the highlight of Gala Day in September 1907 in the town. Those bulky wooden looking life jackets do not appear to be capable of saving anyone's life but rest assured they were. Despite their appearance they were made from cork and were not as heavy as they appear. The funds from this event were destined for the Royal National Lifeboat Institution. The launching of the boat on to the River Wye attracted many enthusiastic spectators. The crew took up their positions accompanied by the Mayor, Alderman Vernon, and the Vicar of High Wycombe and to the delight of the crowd, many of whom volunteered to help, the

The Church Service, the singing, the Carnival, the events on the Rye, which also included children's sports and a hockey match, were a fitting prelude to the evening's events. It seemed according to one observer that the whole of Wycombe had gathered on Tom Burt's Hill and on Marlow Hill to await a torchlight procession which had set out from the Rye to be followed by a firework display and the lighting of a huge bonfire. The lights of the procession viewed from these vantage points would have the appearance of a snake-like line as it wound its way up the hill. The half hour firework display was described as 'dazzling screens of aerial coruscations' and a 'scintillating cascade of multi coloured stars' as rockets, shells, roman candles, golden fountains, silver snakes and 'almost every kind of firework devised by human ingenuity'. The atmosphere was one of joy, good humour and excitement AND romance. The local newspaper reported that young couples took advantage of the shadows to indulge in 'sentimental tete-a-tete'. Then followed the bonfire and to end a busy day for the Carnival Queen and the people of the town there was a dance in the Town Hall attended by over five hundred people with music by Sydney Jerome and his Band. What a day for George V and Queen Mary, for Queen Edith and for all those who celebrated this Silver Jubilee in High Wycombe.

Bottom: A busy group of people beavering away at the tables are members of the pioneering High Wycombe Old Age Pensioners' Association. This scheme, started in 1955, aimed to be a stable and self-supporting workshop for 50 old people and was the brainchild of Mrs M Parry-Jones. She was convinced there was a need for this workshop because although there were schemes run by firms for their retired workers, there was no provision for those with no real skills and nothing to occupy their time. Something far sighted and innovative such as this needed help and the local newspaper immediately gave wonderful support. The association was offered the old Oakley Church Hall for two days each week. All it had to do was pay for heating and lighting. On the first day Mrs Parry-Jones had 80 applications to join. To implement good ideas often needs a little luck. Another newspaper ran a story; a reader thought it was a good idea and gave £2000 to buy and equip a workshop of its own. Within six months

this was done. The new HQ was in Easton Street. Workdays went up to four and the number of workers doubled. What did the workers do? Everything. They packed vacuum cleaner 'Disposall' bags for Hoover; they made Christmas decorations for London's Regent Street; they mailed literature for local firms; they 'Backed Britain'; they ran a stall in the market and much more. The workers were paid at the rate of one shilling (5p) per hour. The scheme worked thus: jobs taken on were paid for at the same rate as the same jobs in the factory, plus a bonus to allow for the saving of factory overheads. That money went to the Association funds which were used for the Association and its workers.

Left: All good things come to an end, unfortunately. The High Wycombe scheme was one. By 1975 after twenty fulsome years it was set to close. The number of pensioners had dwindled and the requisite number of fifty to do the work could not be guaranteed; in fact they were often as low as twenty. Times had brought change. Where at one time old people would come to the centre to meet other people, many were now living in flats with wardens and dayrooms which were generally equipped to undertake lots of various activities. Buckinghamshire County Council was to open an Occupational Therapy Unit mainly for disabled but which the High Wycombe Pensioners could attend and undertake similar work, unpaid of course. There were mixed feelings among the members ranging from missing a free dinner to not wishing to be regarded as disabled to giving it a chance. By July of that year came the inevitable news; the scheme was to close. It had served its purpose at a time when it was needed.

Left: No matter where you lived in this country, Victory in Europe (VE) Day in May 1945 followed a common theme. After all the feelings were the same. The war is over. We should celebrate and it was appropriate that the centre of attention should be given to Britain's future, the children. These children in Liston Hall in Marlow, probably like thousands of other children in this land, sat down at specially decorated tables of red, white and blue to a tea of blancmange, jellies, pastries, potted meat sandwiches, iced cakes decorated with maybe a Victory V and anything else rustled up in those days of rationing. Games would be played, a Tug of War would test the strength of the lads, races would be run and there would be prizes of chocolate and sweets, precious commodities in those days. Entertainment would be provided, maybe even a Punch and Judy show. Songs would be sung and more than likely children would perform, with a great deal of blushing and feigned reluctance, their party pieces. And to go home there would be an orange and a bar of chocolate and a real treat - chewing gum.

Above: Like many other children these children of Baker Street held their VE party in the street. So out came the tables the chairs and the red, white and blue and the celebrations began. The town itself seemed to be one street party. Wycombe Marsh had three parties all due to the hard work of adults and the generosity of local tradesmen. For the children in lower Abercromby Avenue the high spot of their party was Master Dowdy's imitation of Churchill and a Mr Duncan posing as Hitler and somehow being 'hung', much to the delight of the children. There were celebrations everywhere. The town's main buildings were floodlit, street decorations abounded and crowds gathered on the Rye and on the Desborough recreation ground where they were entertained by bands. Dancing in Easton Street was the scene of a 'free-for all party'. It started with a few couples dancing in the street and on the footpath to music from a nearby house. The number of dancers increased as did the number of musicians and soon all the members of a dance band were setting the pace and the rhythm to this happy impromptu entertainment. To add to the occasion the merry making was interspersed with a display of fireworks. Easton Street was obviously the place to be, although everyone will have their own memories on how they spent VE Day and that night!

The faces of the children and adults at this VE party in St Andrew's Church Hall in Gordon Road tell it all. After six years of war, peace in Europe has been secured and the nightmares of bombings, air raids and families caught up in that bloody conflict are almost over. On this great day the celebrations were nationwide and these children were not going to be left out. All the population had taken some time to come to terms with the fact that Germany had surrendered. It was known on Monday, May 7th and announced to the nation the following day. Out came the bunting and flags; shops, businesses and houses were festooned with red, white and blue. In some places even kerbstones were painted in those colours. The celebrations had begun. For these all these children and the adults there was a universal sigh of relief that the war was over. All it needed now was for fathers, husbands and brothers to come home safely, whilst not forgetting that there was still a war to finish on what appeared to be then the other side of the world.

Left: The vast increase in the 1950s and 60s in commercial and private traffic led to town centres becoming more and more clogged up. High Wycombe suffered from this as much as any other town and more than most, for it bore the brunt of traffic a lot of which the M40 now carries. This accident in the High Street outside Sweetlands, the photographers, and the congestion on the High Street may not have been the result of that increase. After all there were crashes when the street contained a small percentage of the vehicles we can see here but it does give an indication of the strain the street and the other main roads in the town had to endure. No wonder there was a documentary film made at this time called 'The Town that Nearly Died of Traffic'. Cliff Michelmore made very good job of explaining High Wycombe's predicament. The bystanders here had a good view of the proceedings and like many other people would wonder how on earth did that saloon car manage to get itself embedded under the Co-operative Wholesale Society Milk lorry. That policeman interviewing one of the drivers presumably will have the answer. We, however, shall have to surmise.

Above: Crowds gather outside the library on Queen Victoria Road waiting the arrival of Her Majesty the Queen to High Wycombe as part of her eight hour visit to Buckinghamshire. Her plan was to arrive at the Town Hall at 10.10am and cram a visit in, including a visit to the Royal Grammar School to celebrate the four hundredth anniversary of receiving its royal charter, before leaving at 11.11am. A lot to do and a lot of people to meet. So it was an early breakfast for the people of High Wycombe if they wanted to see the Queen on this April day in 1962. Schoolchildren with their Union Jacks and members of the Armed Forces took up their places on the route. The crowds were particularly thick outside the Town Hall. Once the cordon was broken but all were shepherded back by 'smiling policemen'. At the Town Hall the Queen received High Wycombe's traditional welcome - an archway of chairs. This she was particularly interested in as it was the custom to place the chairs across the High Street at the Guildhall. Traffic on the A40 made that impracticable. She was introduced to civic leaders by the Mayor, Councillor Douglas Hann, and among those present were 17 schoolchildren representing local schools, including Erica Mitchell from Mill End Girls' School and Brian Taylor from the Boys' School of the same name. A very exciting and memorable day for those two children and all the others.

Above: The crowds had to take every opportunity to gain a good vantage point to see the Royal visitor whether it was from the pavement, an office window, up a tree or a lamp post. Her Majesty had received as a memento of her visit a wooden carved jewel casket made in the town. The bells of the Parish Church rang out as the Queen set out through the town for her visit to the Royal Grammar School. Here she was met by two lines of boys in Combined Cadet Force uniform and was greeted in the Hall by five hundred boys, governors, masters and their wives. The Queen toured the school where she was able to view the building work going on as the school expanded and she showed a keen interest in the new Science block and the dining room. Soon her thirty-five minute visit to the school was over and like all plans that need a strict timetable the Queen's visit was running late but not before she granted the boys, and their teachers, an extra day's holiday.

Right: The Guard of Honour for this Royal visit in the sunshine was provided by the 1st Green Jackets, 43rd and 52nd. The formalities of any royal visit are detailed and extensive. They are often a necessary encumbrance especially at the time, for the days of royal walkabouts were yet to come. But it is the informalities which people remember from the motorist who wanted to drive up Marlow Hill and could not understand why not, to the little girl who in an effort to get a closer look had her foot accidentally trodden on by a policeman, and the VIP who could not get the boot of his official car unlocked. Tragedy - his bowler hat was inside. But he was saved. A local policeman had the know-how. His hat was retrieved and the VIP was correctly attired. A memorable day for the Mayor, for those presented to Her Majesty and for the crowds who waited so long and so enthusiastically for even a glimpse of the Queen, and again a great day for High Wycombe.

The building blocks of success

The company, I L Beeks (HW) Limited as it is now known, was originally set up well over 30 years ago in 1965 and has already accrued an interesting history. The company was established under the name S D Fountain and Partners Limited. The S D Fountain of the name being, Sidney Dennis Fountain and his 'Partner' being Ivor Leonard Beeks.

Sidney Dennis Fountain had spent the early part of his career gaining valuable experience by working as a bricklayer. Before establishing his partnership with Ivor, Sidney was living at 96 Cressex Road and working as a builder and contractor.

Ivor Leonard Beeks came from a family which has a history of building going back over four generations. His great-grandfather built many houses in South Wales and several of his uncles were prominent in the industry locally. Indeed, Ivor himself acknowledges that, 'Behind every successful man is a good family'! Unlike his great-grandfather Ivor Beeks is a native of High Wycombe and was born in the town in 1941. He attended the former Wycombe Technical Institute in Easton Street and later completed an approved part time course in Building. The subjects in his final examination included: Mathematics; Technology; Science; History of Building and Structure of the Industry; and Book Keeping all of which he passed on 1st August 1963 and was awarded an Ordinary National Certificate in Building. Before entering into partnership with Sidney, Ivor worked as a surveyor with Y J Lovell and then left that company for subsequent employment with the local authorities of Wycombe Rural District Council and Marlow Urban District Council before leaving to start his own business drawing plans for buildings.

Above: The Memorandum and Articles of Association for the firm of S D Fountain & Partners Ltd, formed in 1965. Right: Ivor's grandparents outside the premises at New Road, Booker.

It was while securing his first job to tender that Ivor met Sidney. Sidney had also tendered for the same small job and in fact went ahead and completed the work. The men realised that it would be better if they joined forces rather than working in competition with each other and the agreement to become partners in business was made.

S D Fountain and Partners Limited was established on 3rd August 1965 and registered as a private company under Section 28 of the Companies Act of 1948. The objectives for which the company was established were many, in fact 25 different objects were officially listed! Amongst others they included, 'To undertake the erection, construction, decoration, repair, cleansing and finishing of buildings, erections, constructions and works of all kinds' as well as, 'To manufacture, buy, sell and otherwise deal in glass, pottery, earthenware, bricks, stone, pipes, slates, tiles, concrete, lime, cement, plaster, timber, steel, iron ....', the list goes on. Indeed, it is a wonder how the partners decided where to start! The share capital of the new company was £1000 which was divided into 1000 shares of £1 each! The first Directors of the company were named as, Sidney Dennis Fountain and his wife Lynda Winifred Fountain, and Ivor Leonard Beeks and his future wife Janet Hetherington. Their duty was to run the company; however, they could be

disqualified at any time if they committed any of six listed offences, including becoming of unsound mind!

Fortunately, for the future of what was to become I L Beeks (HW) Limited, the Directors managed not to be found of unsound mind although it is possible that when building up the business they did at times feel like they were! The two young men with their will to succeed, could now begin to do so. They started S D Fountain and Partners Limited from very small works and at first on maintenance. They began by operating from a house in Cressex Road but were soon able to move to a disused garage in New Road, Booker. Indeed, with the help and assistance of Ivor Beeks' parents, who at that time owned the property at Cressex Parade, the area was to be the company's business home for over 15 years.

The High Wycombe Building Contractors and Developers experienced a substantial amount of initial success and only a year or two after establishing the company, S D Fountain and Partners Limited became Registered House Builders. In fact, the company was one of the first companies to

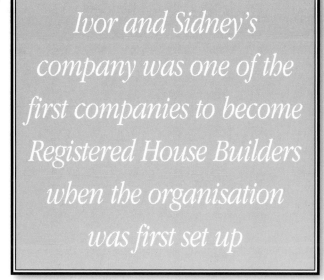

Ivor and Sidney's company was one of the first companies to become Registered House Builders when the organisation was first set up

become Registered House Builders when the organisation was first set up. The mortgage companies had decided that unless building companies were registered they could not have a mortgage without being supervised by a Chartered Surveyor, so the organisation was established and it was a sensible move by the partners to join. Indeed, the partners did not stop there and later also became members of the Federation of Master Builders and Federation of Building Trade Employees.

The 1970s proved to be an eventful decade for S D Fountain and Partners Limited. During this time the company embarked upon building one of its first flat developments. Belmont Mews Resident's Association was completed by the company who subsequently became the landlord of the Association. In 1976, Gordon Lacey joined the company. He was to become an important member of the team and indeed, Ivor later described him as being 'a tower of strength when delicate situations arise, placid and diplomatic' in his role as Contracts Director. In that same year Ivor Beeks showed his own special

Below: *The conversion and construction of four brick and flint cottages at Downley.*

keenness for restoration when his company transformed an old tithe barn near Hughenden. The barn was painstakingly restored and converted and Ivor himself and his family moved into the distinctive home. The successful completion of this project later led to the undertaking of another scheme involving the restoration of barns. The four barns situated at Four Ashes, Terriers, dated from as far back as 1704 and were formerly used for stabling, grain storage and as a milking parlour. They were stripped to leave all the original timber framing, and the

conversion produced four residential homes of great character and appeal with timber framed walls, ceiling beams, exposed brickwork and inglenook fireplaces.

The most significant event of the mid 70s was, however, the departure of Sidney Dennis Fountain from the business. Sidney had increasingly found the high pressures of the company difficult to cope with, and eventually he decided to leave the business bearing his name which he had helped to set up.

Sidney's departure created an exciting opportunity for Ivor Leonard Beeks and the ambitious Ivor seized his chance and bought Sidney's shares, thus becoming the sole owner of the company. This change in ownership was duly marked by a change in the name of the company. This new name, I L Beeks (HW) Limited, was chosen in order to

*Top: The interior structure of the Barns at Four Ashes. **Above:** Lane End Sawmills before development to an Industrial Park.*

commemorate a new chapter in the history of the company and indeed, the company is still known by this name today.

The newly named company continued to flourish under Ivor Beeks and its innovative approach was upheld. Indeed, in the year 1979 to 1980, whilst other developers were letting their newly built premises, I L Beeks (HW) Limited tried something different. The company, which was already active in the field of building for industrial use, became involved in the introduction of owner occupation in industrial development in High Wycombe. Amongst two of the many of these developments undertaken by the company, that had found ready purchasers for their units were, the Lane End Industrial Park and the Desborough Park Industrial Estate.

The year 1982 brought with it a significant event that was to play a memorable part in the history of I L Beeks (HW) Limited. This notable event was the restoration of The Old Court House. The century old former courthouse was built in 1876 and remained in use as a county magistrates court and police station until Wycombe's new law courts were opened in 1974. Ivor's company carefully restored the courthouse, preserving its original character. It also converted the building into prestige offices, and the old courtroom itself was divided into four sections. The Old Courthouse restoration was completed and officially reopened in the year 1982. Mr H S Ross, who was at the time an Assistant Chief Constable in the Thames Valley Police, performed the opening ceremony for the Wycombe security firm, Risk Management Services Limited, who had purchased part of the building as part of their expansion programme. This event was so significant for I L Beeks (HW) Limited however, because the transformed local landmark, The Old Courthouse, was later to become the base for the firm when it moved there from its old premises. The courthouse became the nerve centre for the Beeks group and alongside the modern offices, fitted with the very latest hi-tech equipment, a planning and design centre was installed which

Left: A snowy scene of the barns at Four Ashes prior to their conversion. Below: The completion of the conversion of the barns at Four Ashes.

played an important role in the wide ranging services in the building industry.

The success of I L Beeks (HW) Limited meant that Ivor himself was in a position to be able to indulge some of his interests outside the building trade. In 1986, whilst on holiday in Portugal, Ivor was invited to meet with Wycombe Wanderers Football Club. This meeting led to Ivor being given the opportunity to indulge his interest in football. At the time Wycombe Wanderers was a non-league club run by a management committee. The club desperately wanted to gain league status and Ivor Beeks was the man to help this happen. Ivor accepted the offer to be appointed a Director and then Chairman of the club. Indeed, since Ivor's initial involvement in Wycombe Wanderers Football Club, the team has now managed to attain league status and is now in the second division!

The year 1989 was an important one for I L Beeks (HW) Limited. By this year as well as having his wife Janet already working as an active Director within the company, Ivor had been joined in the business by his eldest son Mark. At that time Mark was engaged in controlling the carpentry work on site. Ivor and Janet's other children Paul and Sarah were still busy in their studies. Paul was studying to be a surveyor at Brighton Polytechnic whilst Sarah was taking her 'A' Level examinations at Wycombe's Lady Verney High School. Whilst all this was going on, it was also in the same year that I L Beeks (HW) Limited completed another first. The 6th March 1989 was an equally important day for High Wycombe as it was for I L Beeks (HW) Limited. For, it was on this day that the first new luxury hotel to be built in the town's centre for over 100 years was opened. Ivor Beeks came up with the idea to build a new hotel in 1987, and it took only two years before his idea came to fruition with the opening of the Alexandra Hotel.

The idea came to him whilst he was driving home from North Bucks. On the journey home he realised that High Wycombe urgently needed further hotel bedroom space and decided then and there to pursue ways and means of meeting this need. The

Above: A company letterhead from the late 1970s.
Below: Rye Mill Factory prior to development of The Millstream luxury flats.

> *Brickwork has become a craft again with bands and panels set into buildings to make them more interesting*

new hotel was an entirely new construction, purpose built with every modern facility, rather than the conversion of an existing building. Although Ivor had considerable experience in the building trade he acknowledged the fact that hotels were something of which he had little previous knowledge except of a recreational kind! Luckily, Alain Thibault, a great friend and colleague, had a vast amount of knowledge of the hotel trade and agreed to lend his expertise to the project from day one. Alain was a trainee manager at London's prestigious Savoy Hotel from 1962 to 1965 after which he came to High Wycombe as the very last manager of the town's famous old Red Lion Hotel and when this was closed he became the Chief executive of Concorde Hotels. With Alain's help, Ivor and his company completed the construction of The Alexandra Hotel in Queen Alexandra Road on a

11,783 square feet site near Bucks College and directly opposite Wycombe General Hospital. The hotel was officially opened by the Mayor and Mayoress of High Wycombe then, Mohammed and Valerie Razzaq. Almost immediately it became an instant success and managed to surpass all expectations in restaurant function and hotel reservations.

The year 1990 was yet another important one in the history of the company. It was in this year that I L Beeks (HW) Limited celebrated its 25th anniversary. This milestone in the history of the company was marked with a celebration dinner at Ye Olde Bell Hotel, Hurley on 18th May for the employees of the business and other guests. When asked about his thoughts on the last 25 years of trading in High Wycombe Ivor said of the town that 'it is a very challenging town with great scope for improvement, which is what we are seeing today both in the change of the centre and design ... Brickwork has become a craft again with

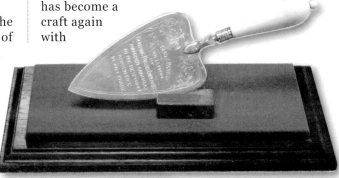

Above: *The silver trowel awarded to the best apprentice, Nicholas Smith.* **Below:** *The steelwork construction of Park House Office, Desborough Park Business Centre.*

bands and panels set into buildings to make them more interesting'. Another highly praised and successful project changing the centre of the town, undertaken by the company throughout its 25 years, was the Millstream in London Road, High Wycombe. This project tastefully used modern materials to produce a blend of old and new architecture in one of the town's most attractive areas, adjacent to the Rye. Another project completed by the 25th anniversary did not run quite as smoothly as was expected. The project for the construction of the Central Park Business Centre at Bellfield Road in High Wycombe took a total of three years of planning applications and an appeal to the Minister for the Environment before permission to go ahead was granted! The completed development comprised industrial units offering flexible accommodation to suit a variety of occupiers.

The success of I L Beeks (HW) Limited did not slow down after reaching its 25th anniversary. Indeed, the business continued to thrive. The company has

Above both pictures: *The Alexandra Hotel during construction and following completion.*
Below: *The official opening of the Alexandra Hotel in March 1989. The Mayor and Mayoress of High Wycombe Mohammed and Valerie Razzaq officially open the hotel with director Alain Thibault, centre and Ivor Beeks, left.*

won several Merit Awards for projects in High Wycombe and was awarded yet another one during this time. I L Beeks has always maintained a belief in training its staff and has taken on many apprentices throughout the years. Indeed, it was one of the company's apprentices, Nicholas Smith, who was awarded the title of Best Craft Apprentice in Any Trade by the Aylesbury and District Association of Building Trades Employers, and accordingly presented with a silver trowel. Since 1990 the building and restoration work side of I L Beeks has also continued to flourish. In 1999 the company demolished Lacey Green village hall in order to build a new building in its place. The villagers had raised £167,000 over two years for this project and when this sum was matched by the Millennium Fund they were able to enlist I L Beeks to replace the village hall. Other projects undertaken at this time were the refurbishment of an old thatched cottage; the building of a new pavilion for the cricket club; and £1 million worth of works to the Union Baptist Church.

Ivor Beeks' company has come a long way since its establishment in 1965. The company has now moved from The Old Courthouse but, coincidentally the new base in Archway House looks across to the courthouse and serves as a relevant reminder to the employees of part of the company's history and

work! Ivor's son, Mark, has now worked his way up to becoming the Contracts Director of the company and his younger son, Paul, has also joined the business where he works as an Estimating Director. As I L Beeks (HW) Limited moves forward towards its 50th year Ivor intends to continue with his 'crusade' to put something back into the town where he was born. Indeed, the company is not content to rest on its laurels, and no doubt the Beeks family innovative thinking and entrepreneurial spirit will ensure that High Wycombe benefits from many more worthy I L Beeks (HW) Limited developments in the future.

Top left: *Mark Beeks.*
Left: *The company directors outside Archway House, from left to right Philip Mason, Mark Beeks, Steve Wallington, Paul Beeks and Ivor Beeks.*

At leisure

It seems it is almost 'girls only day' at the Fryer's Mill Swimming Pool. The costumes and bathing caps certainly have a uniform look to them rather different from the fashions of today. But it is recreation, and for those children it was a real luxury. They have some kind of changing facility and a chance to make the best of the water. A question to be asked could be 'How many of these children could swim?' After all we today expect the vast majority of our youngsters to be able to swim and there are opportunities from many sources for them to learn and practise. The facilities for swimming and recreation between the two world wars were limited in all towns. The original swimming pool for the people of High Wycombe was situated at the West End Recreation Ground on West Wycombe Road. The pool was fed by water from the River Wye but had to be closed in 1947 by the council because of the danger of pollution. A new pool was built on the Rye on the site of an old Roman villa in 1957. High Wycombe was more fortunate than most; it did have the Rye.

Above: The Boating Pool on the Rye was situated on the town side of the children's playground near the swings. It contained a stream with its own little waterfall fed from the Wye River. The playground itself was provided by H J Cox, a wholesale tobacconist and former mayor, while the paddling pool was owed to the generosity of Councillor J Gibson. It had swings, a butterslide, roundabouts and seesaws. There was the boating pool and the famous and treasured Dyke, an aquatic adventure playground where you could hire boats. Here and on the river you could sail little boats or make your own raft or find an old tyre and be a pirate. There were seasons for games - tadpoles season, skipping season, marbles season, conker season. There was a definite demarcation between soccer and cricket seasons and boys did not cross that time line, A child's life was very much less complicated than today's and childhood pastimes lasted longer then, it seemed.

Above right: The Rye, the 'jewel in the town's crown', the much prized and jealously guarded open area for all the town's recreational activities, formal and informal. A scheme in the 1960s to build a road across the north-west corner of the Rye was successfully opposed by the then Rye Protection Society which grew into the High Wycombe Society. For the children of the town it was one adventure playground. One of the great characters of the Rye was known affectionately to all the children as Uncle Tom. He was a paid supervisor or park keeper, resplendent in his sailor's hat, black jumper white sea socks and wellington boots, although some can recall an astrakhan collar. Reputed to be an ex-actor, Uncle Tom was a great favourite with the children. He lived at Marlow Bottom and was even a popular figure on the bus he caught to work every day. It is said that at one time the council decided to sack him but they reckoned without 'Child Power'. Protests followed, banners were made, the Municipal Offices, if not besieged, were certainly made aware AND it was successful. Uncle Tom was reinstated. Out of such truths legends are made.

There are one or two empty seats with the ominous demand for silence but the need for extra space is glaringly obvious. After being here in Church Street since 1875 this is the last day of the High Wycombe Library. The original intention then was that the Library should be supported from charitable sources and public and private donations. By 1920, however, it was proving extremely difficult to fund it this way. It was obvious then that it would need official support from the ratepayers of the town so it exchanged the word Free for Public in its name. The growth of elementary and secondary education and the development of new technical skills meant that the demand for books and other sources of information grew rapidly after the war. A more literate population was emerging, enjoying novels, devouring reference books and libraries had to cope. High Wycombe was no exception. The old library was not able to cope. It was already sharing its premises with the museum. New premises were needed and in 1935 the new High Wycombe Library took its place with other civic buildings in Queen Victoria Road. So these people in their hunger for the written word will be able to enjoy the specialist facilities and the extra space of a new building. No wonder there was a queue stretching up the road as far as the High Street corner on the first day.

Above: Story time in 1935 for some very attentive young children of High Wycombe as they listen to Miss Lilian Hurd, Borough Librarian, read to them. The new library was able to provide for all literary needs of its users and children were to be no exception. The demand for books matched the growth in popular education; children, more literate and better educated, developed a thirst for novels and during the 1930s a new batch of writers of fiction emerged to match the well established group including R L Stevenson and R Blackmore. But all books in those days looked the same from the outside! Never judge a book by its cover is a truism but the old books did seem to look alike. It took new writers like Enid Blyton and Richmal Crompton to become everyone's friend. Their eagerly awaited colourful books were collected and swapped like stamps.

The children's library was now an essential part of many children's lives. That is how these children would learn to appreciate the fine heritage of English Literature; to read for pleasure; to value language and help them gain a better understanding of the world in which they lived. There continued to be many fine authors of children's fiction. Thank goodness the tradition lives on.

This vast area of space in the Rye in High Wycombe was the scene of much of the children's recreational life. They lived in an unsophisticated world where sailing boats, rolling hoops, spinning tops, collecting tiddlers and tadpoles, making dens, getting their feet wet were day-long exercises. Hours could be spent on the seesaw and the slide and the round-about and the climbing frame and the rocking horse. There were several versions of impro-vised games of chasing and capturing. This and much more is what the Rye offered the children of the town. That is why it was always regarded as precious. Children and adults needed space; houses with gardens were few and far between. Facilities for organised games were limited. Land was privately owned and often jealously guarded . Whoever gave the Rye to the town and those who provided facilities showed great foresight. It was an asset and it still is.

Around the town centre

The usual view of High Street is to look westwards towards the Guildhall but on this occasion this 1930s view is away from that building, looking at the Red Lion, one of the great coaching inns in the country with, at its peak, stabling for forty-two horses. From its balcony Disraeli and in 1945 Churchill made great political speeches. Churchill's was not as long or as passionate as Disraeli's oration of over one and a quarter hours. Roberts, the photography shop, was reputed to be the oldest shop in the town and the only one to retain its jettied upper storeys and timber frames. The tobacconists below had for many years Mrs Cutter serving customers. Often we associate the face behind the counter with the name of the shop. Shop and server were synonymous. The Grapes Inn is now Boots and the Imperial Stores above the Red Lion soon was to become International Stores. The significance of the some of the buildings in High Street can be gleaned from the fact that several are listed buildings. Guildhall is the obvious one and two others are the premises now occupied by NatWest Bank and those occupied by the Alliance and Leicester. It is a pity that the frontages of buildings here could not be retained in their old form. Some efforts have been made, not, unfortunately, in the case of a largish bank further up the street.

The Queen Anne style Town Hall was built in 1904 and was the first building to be erected on this newly created civic avenue named in honour of Queen Victoria. The road itself ran along the line of the drive to Wycombe Abbey. The Town Hall had a main hall seating originally 1100 people including a gallery. There was a stage and dressing rooms and an organ was intalled a little later. Above the entrance hall was originally the Red Room (now the Oak Room) with its five stained glass windows. Modernisation took place in 1972/3 which shut off the gallery from the main hall and transformed it into a lounge bar. The other buildings in this road, all with a great deal of civic importance, were built very much within the same period this time in neo-Georgian style. In 1931 came the Municipal Offices, then the Library, followed by the Police Station. The police station was a Borough Force until 1947 when the County took over responsibility for that and for other emergency services round about the same time. The road was formerly a carriageway from the High Street to Wycombe Abbey which was never an abbey as such. In 1896 it became a girls' school. For the duration of the second world war it was closed and became the Headquarters of the United States Army Eighth Air Force.

itself was culverted in 1965 as part of the plans for the new Inner Relief Road and shopping centre and much of the rest given to car parking. A line of a song of the 1960s went 'They paved paradise, put up a parking lot'. It may not have been paradise but it certainly had potential!.

Top: Any town or city usually has a civic landmark which is instantly recognisable and peculiar to the town. For some it is the Town Hall, and for others it is a series of buildings, for others it is a feature like an archway. For High Wycombe it would be the Guildhall, standing opposite the Market House. This area, known as the Cornmarket is the historic centre of the town. The Guildhall was one of a sequence of buildings dating back to the eighteenth century and bore the still visible inscription 'Erected in the year of Our Lord 1752 at the expense of John, Earl of Shelburne in the memory of which the Corporation caused this to be written'. Renovations took place in 1859 and latterly in the early 1980s. This whole area of the Market Place bounded by White Hart Street, Church Street and Queen Square contained many of the medieval market stalls. The tradition peculiar to the town of weighing the Mayor on taking office and at the end of his tenure to check whether he had gained weight at the expense of the ratepayers continues to take place outside the Guildhall. The mayor in 1960 weighed in at over 20 stones at the end of his term of office. Had he put on weight or lost some? We wonder.

Above: A photograph of old High Wycombe in 1935 as a bus and car trundle over Newland Bridge chased by a lone pedestrian. Beyond is the National School and across the River Wye Newland Street. The old National School on White Hart Street was established by the Church of England in 1855 catering for 470 children. Eventually, after the Church built a new school, it was converted into Nutt's Auction room and finally into Murray's Department store. Here was the site of the Borough Police Station. Aldridge's shop is on the far side of the bridge and on the right is the Jolly Butcher public house. The area had traditionally housed the families of workers employed in the numerous furniture factories but by this time had become very overcrowded and naturally public health was a growing problem. Everything was to be razed to the ground. The river

A 1929 view of Frogmoor Gardens showing some of the traditional features of the area including the mock Tudor building in the background. The provision of utilities such as electricity was then a civic responsibility and here we see the electricity offices belonging to the borough. The Gardens themselves, originally a patch of marshy ground where the brook came down from Hughenden to meet the Wye, had been donated to the town in 1877 through the generosity of JO Griffits. He had purchased the site and had it laid out in York stone complete with a magnificent fountain and the inevitable but absolutely necessary horse trough. A more ornate baroque fountain replaced the original

in 1895 and remained there until the Second World War when it was removed in the same way as many other metal features in the country to help to sustain the war effort. However there has always been some doubt as to whether the fountain was actually used for the purpose of armament production. By then it had fallen from grace and was no longer a thing of beauty and grace and an object of local pride. It became a neglected eyesore and took on the role of public litter bin. What is certain is that Frogmoor Gardens was for many years special to the town of High Wycombe as a meeting place, and rallying site and the town's own version of Hyde Park Corner.

An aerial photograph of High Wycombe as it was in the 1940s. No shopping centres yet. High Street, as ever, dominates the scene, acting as the backbone of the town with the Guildhall acting as the town's focal point. In the foreground, long before it is culverted, is the River Wye with Newland Bridge providing one crossing point. Would the planners of today have been so ready as those in the 1960s to block the river off here from the town as it is today? Or would they have incorporated the river and bridges and walks into a plan which enhanced rather than obliterated the scene? Churches feature highly in this view; there is the Parish Church, of course, and the White Hart Street Methodist Church - and on Castle Street the Gothic brickwork of St Augustine's R C Church, which stood there until 1955. Near to that church was the tea factory and Hewitt's, basket makers. The Grammar School stands out in the centre background as we make our way towards Queen Victoria Road, containing the town's administrative buildings. Two shops take a prominent place here, McIlroy's and Murray's, both synonymous with the town's commercial life. Certainly a photograph to bring back memories of High Wycombe as it was and cause debate about what was where and when.

Above: The Little Market House known with some affection as the 'Little Pepper Pot' has now dropped the 'Little' from its title. It was the work of Robert Adam, better known for his fireplaces. The more knowledgeable regard this building as not one of his better efforts. To this untrained eye it is one of the town's treasures. Each town possesses something unique which immediately attracts the visitor's eye. Once or twice it is an eyesore but more often a building which is unique. High Wycombe has two unique buildings, this and the Guildhall. No one can think of a shopping centre as appealingly eye-catching no matter how useful they are. The area behind the Little Market House was where pigs were once sold, known as the hog market. The Antelope public house is a very interesting building, architecturally of course. The windows on the first floor, known as Yorkshire Casements, open by sliding sideways. This area of the town is very much part of its history. Town centres are living things not museums to the past, and the history of any town is well worth actively preserving and making good use of.

Left: The name of this street comes from East Town. It once held the town's Post Office with the date 1901 carved into the brickwork on the first floor window. The photographs of the building at the time show that it had style and dignity like many other towns' post offices. It does seem a pity that in many places 'stylish' and 'dignified' when describing some buildings like Post Offices have been sacrificed for 'functional'. In 1934 that office was moved to Queen Victoria Street and now it is hidden away in a shopping centre. Easton Street changed very little before the 1950s when the Almshouses, built in 1680, were demolished and replaced by the Law Courts. At the far end of the street was Taylor's Sweetshop, makers of their own Aunt Anne's Winter Mixture, designed to ward off coughs and colds. Wright's Dairy would be at one time like many of the local dairies in that it would exercise the right to graze two cows free of charge on the Rye. There was a familiar sight of the thirty plus cows unescorted wandering along Easton Street and High Street back to the dairyman each evening. They would be milked, bedded down, milked again next morning after which they would proceed back to the Rye. By 1927 the cows numbering about 30 belonged to two dairymen only! The Wycombe Prep School under the direction of the Misses Thornton and Morris was situated behind the Union Baptist Church until closure in 1967. Here Mr Fred Bailey could provide tuition in Pianoforte, Rhythmic Movement and Percussion. Easton Street, such an important and imposing street, now, unfortunately, can only be described as 'a shadow of its former self'.

Above: The traditional view of High Street in 1939 presents a scene of peace and contentment. The horse and cart cuts a solitary image as the street reflects the national trend in the number of cars and the different makes. It would not have been so long ago that the most common cars, other those in the luxury bracket, were the Austin 10 and the Morris Minor, both priced at between £175 to £200. But cars were beginning to acquire more modern designs. New types of steel were being developed; it became possible to design cars with curved features rather than the box-like construction of earlier models. They had now acquired most of the features familiar to us today. By 1939 there was one car to every twenty-four people and it began to change the pace of life and work for its owner. But the people who had cars were those who could afford them. For others there was the bus or the coach. As towns like High Wycombe expanded and new housing estates were built, there was a need for an efficient public transport system. The coach service was cheaper than the railway so long distance travel meant for more freedom of movement; visits to relatives and to other towns on the 'chara' were now a possibility. But here it is 1939 and there are other matters to concern the people of the town and the country rather than a bus trip or a new car.

Bottom: White Hart Street which leads into High Street takes its name from the White Hart Inn which stood on the right hand side. Originally the street formed one of the sides of the triangle within which the medieval market stood. It was once known as Hog Lane and this led into Newlands which as the name implies was new land on the boundaries of the ancient borough side. Some of the more famous names in the town's commercial life were situated here. Firms such as the aptly named Thorogoods the baker. Ricketts, the butcher, Hick's children's outfitter and the butchers with two pigs outside on the wall, are still there. Interestingly Maypole with Liptons and Home and Colonial were regarded in many towns as local fixtures even though they were part of national chains. Maypole was considered to be one of the more economical stores in which to shop. Later even those three national stores would find it difficult to compete with larger rivals. The competition grew too fierce. So, although they retained their names and individual shopfronts, they did what other companies in other businesses did and became one enterprise called the Home and Colonial Group. It is said that Rivetts were determined to ensure that Marks and Spencer should not gain a foothold in the town. This gave rise to the story that to do this, every time a shop was for sale Rivetts bought it. What Rivetts did do was to found Murrays, the town's own department store which remained until the 1970s until after the Octagon shopping centre was created.

Right: An interesting 1950s view of High Street mainly for the traffic, especially the beginnings of a modern phenomenon, car towing a caravan. They appear to be chasing the luxury saloon eastwards. As traffic increased, the centre of High

Wycombe became busier and busier as it was one of the main routes to the west. Demands would eventually lead to drastic action. Car owning was now spreading to all classes; it gave new freedoms. Holidays and shopping trips were taken by car which was good news for campsite owners and supermarket owners but bad for town centres. It was estimated that for every one per cent of workers who changed to driving there was a twelve per cent increase in vehicles at the busiest parts of the day. The coach parked outside the Falcon Inn is more than likely here destined for Wales. In the 1930s the town was a haven for unemployed Welsh to seek work here where there were job vacancies. It was at one time estimated that there were two thousand Welshmen working in the town. The coach was there to take those who had not settled with their families back to South Wales for the weekend. Even when the furniture trade was beginning to decline there was still this influx looking for work.

Frogmoor contained the town's first cinema, the Palace, built in 1909 showing 'high class vaudeville acts and animated pictures'. Prices were 3d, 6d, 9d, and the best 1/-. How much do we have to pay now? Two performances at 7 and 9pm with a Saturday matinee at 2pm. In the following year it was destroyed by fire and moved next door on to the site of the Swimming Baths where it was known as the Electric Theatre. The new Palace was opened on the other side of Frogmoor in 1920s. Other cinemas in those exciting days in the town were the Rex built in 1912, which once even staged a boxing match, the Grand in Desborough Road built in 1913, the Majestic, later renamed the Odeon, in Castle Street with

> *Frogmoor contained the town's first cinema - the Palace, built in 1909*

its proscenium designed like an oriental palace and with glittering stars in the ceiling. Dennis Nordern, it is said, was the manager there before the war. The present Chilterns shopping centre is on the site of the former Palace Cinema. Some interesting shops and businesses here. Curry's was in all probability a cycle shop at this time. Wycombe Borough Electric Power existed when the responsibility for utilities like water, gas and electricity rested in the hands of the local corporation. It would take some time before that responsibility was centralised. The gentlemen on the bench can sit there and recall what has been and what is occurring here on Frogmoor in 1938 although there are matters of graver national concern at this time.

Left: A 1958 view of High Street which can still cope with the traffic. Cars have no trouble parking and pedestrians none crossing. The Chequers in the background at the corner of Church Street was at one time a timber framed seventeenth century building until it fell foul of developers in the 1970s when no one seemed to want to make a decision about its future. It fell into dereliction. The Chequers now remains only as a reproduction and if nothing else serves as a reminder of what should never happen to a town's building of such stature. On the front left is the garage belonging to Davenport and Vernon who could at this time speak what sounded like a foreign language when it advertised its Tecalemit Lubrication Service, Power Washing and Valeting, Crypton Test Tune Installation and Ferodo-Tapley Brake Testing under road conditions and a special Breakdown Ambulance. Shades of things to come. The garage sold the following makes of new cars; Austin, Hillman, Humber, Rover, Lanchester, Daimler and Commer. Like much of Britain's motor industry a thing of the past. The changes to the High Street as we see it today are not evident here. Soon these shop fronts will change. The new owners of Berry's, the jewellers, were obliged to retain the original shopfront. Today the visitor generally has to look at the first floors to gain some idea of High Wycombe in its splendour. It is a measure of any town's ambition how it copes with change in people's shopping habits, the increase in traffic, the movement away from the individual

service or shop and the take-over by out of town enterprises. For all these changes to it, High Street still manages to retain much of the grandeur seen here.

Below: This 1950s view down High Street towards the Guildhall is the traditional view of the town's principal street and contains some of the most recognisable and finest buildings. The Red Lion, only a replica lion survives, is now Woolworth's. The original frontage has been replaced by arches modelling those at the Guildhall. At this end is the White House Studio of then Sweetland's, THE photographer of High Wycombe for many years. This building has wall-paintings rather than wallpaper painted by the same artist who similarly decorated the Old Golden Cross Public House in Oxford. The White House has a unique method of collecting and dispersing rainwater from the roof via the attic, a feat of engineering too difficult for this layman to explain. The original clock of the Bucks Free Press remains though the building here is used by a building society. As well as publishing the local paper, the Bucks Free Press also published the Jewish Chronicle and just to keep an ecumenical balance the Catholic Herald. The bank at the corner of Corporation Street was the original Wycombe Bank. Think of how many banks there were at this time and where are they now. What happened to the Wycombe Bank? What became of the District, the Provincial, Martins, Westminster, Midland? Swallowed up. At least High Street is still recognisable.

An interesting photograph of corner of Queen Victoria Road in 1950. There are the first signs here of the increase in traffic that would bedevil High Wycombe in future years as private and commercial vehicles take over the streets. The land to build this civic road, originally part of the grounds of Wycombe Abbey, was given to the town by Lord Carrington. The bridge at the south end of the road carries Queen Victoria's name with a plaque recognising this. The stone gate lodge now half way up Marlow Hill called the Rupert Lodge was originally situated here on this corner of the High Street. These gates were rebuilt on Marlow

Hill in 1901 when this civic avenue was constructed. On the opposite corner of Easton Street and Queen Victoria Road stood the old Wycombe Brewery, demolished in 1932 to make way for redevelopment thus giving space for this two way traffic. But on this sunny Spring day there is still time to sit and stare; there is not the hustle of having to get somewhere quickly. Buildings like the Post Office and the Library have an imposing look about them and mix easily with the background and flower garden on the corner. If you took a photograph today from the same viewpoint, would that feeling still be there?

At your service

Below: It is nearly the end of the war and perhaps the High Wycombe Civil Defence Wardens had something to be pleased about for their contribution to the war effort was one of bravery and dedication. Each member here would have his own story to tell and a whole host of memories that would live with him for the rest of his life. They were not the interfering overbearing busybodies played by Bill Pertwee in 'Dad's Army', well not all of them. It is now 1945 and the threat of invasion has long since gone. In the previous year the London Civil Defence was virtually disbanded; blackout gave way to 'dim-out, so no more 'put that light out, don't you know there's a war on?'. On Christmas Day of that year churches were allowed to light their stained glass windows and a few days later car headlight masks were abolished. You could now do things that were once prohibited, like buying a large scale map, using a car radio, releasing racing pigeons without permission and sleeping in an uncamouflaged tent. If you did that a couple of years ago, these gentlemen would be on your tail. However, what the British citizen was still not able to do in 1944 without the threat of prosecution was to 'spread alarm and despondency'. Do that if you dare!

'Dad's Army' they may have been called and the television series of that name has continued to bring into focus the nature of the Home Guard. At first known as the Local Defence Volunteers(LDV), the new name was introduced in July, 1940. Their numbers at this time across the country were a million and a half. Sufficient equipment could not be found for this huge force of part-time militia, comprising men between the ages of seventeen and sixty-five who did not have part-time duty in civil defence. Their uniform was initially a solitary armband but was soon replaced by Denims, the fatigue version of the Army's attire. At first companies would train with a collection of impromptu weapons until shipments of rifles arrived

from America and Canada. The threat of invasion was real and those parts of the country where landings were expected were first to be equipped with uniforms, weapons and equipment. The main purpose of the Home Guard was to meet the threat of enemy parachute troops, an expected feature of any German invasion attempt. Evening training sessions and nightly duties guarding railways, bridges, factories and other important installations in the locality was the Home Guard's lot. The efficiency of units varied from district to district, a lot depending on their Commanders, mostly ex-army officers of the earlier war. 'Dad's Army' painted a very accurate picture, don't you think? These gentlemen in this photograph might agree.

Whether you are supposed to look so contented being in hospital at Christmas time in 1935 is doubtful but when it is considered how well you appear to be looked after then perhaps a little smile of satisfaction is in order. But it is hospital and these ladies are in there for some medical reason. Hospitals at this time were owned and managed by local authorities, or by a charity or privately run for profit. The story of the growth of hospital services in High Wycombe would be little different to any other town. Accommodation for the sick was, and still is of course, a priority

as much as preventing disease. The progress of medical science meant that illnesses and diseases were beginning to be treatable. After the war this progress quickened; the population was growing and every town and city needed to look at what it could offer in terms of hospital facilities. By 1966 High Wycombe possessed the General Hospital which was regarded a fine example of modern hospital design. It was meeting contemporary needs. So was this women's ward in this photograph. Progress means the need to change and High Wycombe responded to that need.

Be prepared! The impact of war was to be felt in every part of this country. At home this country did prepare. Gas masks had been issued to everyone in the previous year, 1938. Anderson shelters were features in every street. Sandbags protected every important building in every town and this one outside High Wycombe Fire Station is a typical example. There was a complete blackout and in the early days accidents increased as pedestrians walked off kerbs, knocked into lamp posts or stepped into the paths of cars. Serious advice given in one place to pedestrians was to wear a white carnation, leave their shirt tails hanging out or failing that carry a white Pekinese dog. It was more than serious; it was deadly. Official calculations anticipated that 100,000 tons of bombs would fall on London in the first fourteen days and High Wycombe was not that far from London. This dire warning was added to by the threat of the use of poison gas against us. Like every other person involved at home, volunteer or otherwise, this fireman is going to have a very busy war.

Above: The Gas Company Fire team of 1944 lined up left to right as follows;- Tommy Morris, Jim Simmonds, C Bowls, Bill Sutton, Ernie Irons, Robert Wheeler with the Mayor of High Wycombe, Councillor C L Fry. The organisation of emergency services during the war was rather piecemeal in that there was a mixture of the professionals and volunteers and in the case of companies, especially such a major utility one like a Gas Company, it was imperative that it was prepared. Too often especially in the early years, equipment was woefully inadequate. Families were encouraged to buy for 12/6 a stirrup pump designed to enable one person with a bucket of water and some sand to put out one fire. Even as late as June 1945, 95,000 of these were still on order. Bombs rained down on this country for most of the years of the war and fire fighters were always in the thick of action. It is said that firemen have to rush into places others try to rush out from. The threats of V1 flying bombs, doodlebugs or buzz bombs and rockets were only too much of a reality for much of this country. The destruction of life and property nationwide was devastating. Almost too late was the realisation that our emergency services would need to be realistically equipped and it is with some pride and a great deal of relief that these men have now this new machine.

Shopping spree

The Queen's Square in the 1930s is not much different from today's part of the town . It has, as is said in another context, 'kept its shape'. The view to the Parish Church here is as grand as today's. What has changed are the shops. The mixture of local shops and the larger national chains is evident here. The newcomers such as Lyon's Tea Shop and Woolworths were accepted as part of a town's commercial life. They fitted in with George's Ironmongers and Gunsmiths and Cousin's Outfitters and Milward's Shoes.

It was a tolerable mixture. The range of goods on offer was increasing; new foods were being introduced. By this time J Lyons could offer to the public coffee, once considered a luxury, as well as tea. On offer were a range of blends brought about by grinding and mixing various types of bean, principally from Africa and South America. Coffee became affordable but it was not until 1937 that instant coffee was first marketed and that was in America. We had to wait a few years for that to appear in our shops.

Fire Alarm corner is an intriguing name for a shop on Church Street although the motor cycle and sidecar are a sign of times. McIlroy's as ever in those days occupies a very prominent position on this sunny day with the Free Library next door and Woolworth's on the other side. For those of us who wish to be further intrigued the Hairdressers is offering a shimnel, which is a short layered cut, a marcel, which is a steam perm, as well as the more obvious permanent waving. By this time hairdressing became something of an art form. The short bobs were being replaced with long wavy hair often permed into curls. The use of hair shampoo became increasingly more widespread. Blame Hollywood. Film stars were used to advertise products like 'Drene' the 'Shampoo of the Stars'. Patricia Roc would agree that 'no other shampoo leaves your hair looking so glamorous' as Drene. For men, hair dressings in the form of oils and creams became popular; the smooth swept back look became THE fashion. The stylish young men in High Wycombe now competed with the young ladies to have elegance in hairdressing. The young of today are not the trendsetters they think they are!

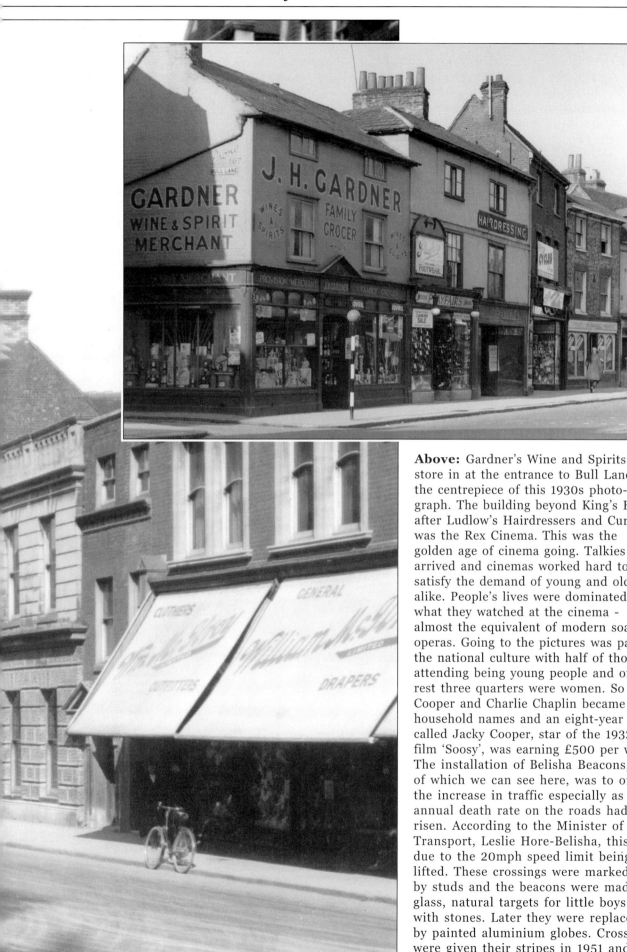

Above: Gardner's Wine and Spirits store in at the entrance to Bull Lane is the centrepiece of this 1930s photograph. The building beyond King's Head after Ludlow's Hairdressers and Curry's was the Rex Cinema. This was the golden age of cinema going. Talkies had arrived and cinemas worked hard to satisfy the demand of young and old alike. People's lives were dominated by what they watched at the cinema - almost the equivalent of modern soap operas. Going to the pictures was part of the national culture with half of those attending being young people and of the rest three quarters were women. So Gary Cooper and Charlie Chaplin became household names and an eight-year old called Jacky Cooper, star of the 1932 film 'Soosy', was earning £500 per week. The installation of Belisha Beacons, one of which we can see here, was to offset the increase in traffic especially as the annual death rate on the roads had risen. According to the Minister of Transport, Leslie Hore-Belisha, this was due to the 20mph speed limit being lifted. These crossings were marked out by studs and the beacons were made of glass, natural targets for little boys with stones. Later they were replaced by painted aluminium globes. Crossings were given their stripes in 1951 and the beacons became plastic and began to 'wink' in 1952. There does not seem a traffic problem here though.

The Fifty Shilling Tailors is being drastically undercut by Maxwell's sale where a man's suit is a pound cheaper. It is reputed that this shop had a permanent sale. The Fifty Shilling Tailors was established during the 1920s supplying affordable gentlemen's suits, primarily for ex-servicemen who had fought in the war. The sum of 50/-, two pounds fifty pence in today's currency, would have paid for a very serviceable suit of clothes, a must for any man being interviewed for a job, particularly as a salesman or clerk. In the 1950s, the full name of Fifty Shillings Tailor was abbreviated to FST. Later the firm was taken over by John Collier's, 'the Window to Watch'. Men's

clothing shops sprang up rivalling local outfitters. Soon there came Hepworths, Hornes, Austin Reed, Montague Burtons, the 'Tailor of Taste', and for those with more than fifty shillings Hector Powe. So whenever a man, and his wife, went shopping for his new suit there was always plenty of choice. The Hen and Chickens remains on the building which is now occupied by Dorothy Perkins. Lansdales chemists has retained its original function even today, except it is now called a pharmacy. World's Stores has lost out, however, to a Building Society from Yorkshire soon to follow recent trends and become a bank.

In the 1930s it is estimated that there were ten million cyclists in Britain

Bicycles outnumber cars in this April 1933 photograph of Church Street. Horse drawn traffic was disappearing fast and for many the cycles were still the principal form of transport, especially for getting to and from work. At this time it is estimated there were in Britain ten million cyclists. On the right is the facade of McIlroy's famous department store and the British School which in 1876 had become the town's Free Library until the new one was built in 1935. McIlroy's dominated this corner with Priory Road for many years although on the actual corner stood Turner's, the wholesale and retail stationer, later to become G E Stevens, coal and corn merchants. Eventually Stevens sold it to Marks and Spencers and then the present building was built. The partnership between local firms and nationals, however uneasy, did endure during this period. It was after the war that the nationals began to make giant inroads into the commercial heart of towns. They could buy and sell goods more cheaply. Marks and Spencer and many others took over where local shops could not compete. Any high street in any town is today a predictable collection of the same shops. That is what the modern customer appears to want!

This little girl seems to be rather apprehensive about the photographer outside this shop in Desborough Avenue. After all it is the 1930s and having your photograph taken in the street may not have been a common occurrence. Perhaps she is wondering whether to go and spend her pennies in the shop or whether the other little girl is still her friend. In such a small community everyone knows everyone else and the shop was very much part of that community. There was not the choice or diversity that shoppers demand today. These family owned shops had yet to compete with multi-nationals. They were a centre of life, a place to buy all your goods, a version of the supermarket with more personal service. There is a beginning of a soon to grow trend in the sign which states that Crawley's shop is an agent for Ark food products. Some things don't change much. The other advertisements are familiar though, whether you wish to buy chocolate or tea, cocoa or cigarettes - one or two of those are still around. So young lady, spend your money in there; there is bound to be a choice. A difficult one perhaps between humbugs, black bullets, barley sugars, lemon or pear drops, dolly mixtures or a sherbet dab. What a choice!

At work

In 1937 there began massive improvements to the town centre as the volume of traffic increased and streets like Crendon Street were far too narrow to cope. It was widened to create a wide flared exit to High Street and to Queen Victoria Road. All the properties on the west side of the road were demolished and replaced by the neo-Georgian buildings there today. One of the casualties was the Dial House which possessed a glazed back dial. It was decided to preserve the dial on the south facing walls as a memento and keep it in the museum, but it was delivered in several pieces and thus impossible to restore - only photographs remain.

The tower here is of Christ Church on the east side of the road. It was built to the design of Arthur Vernon for a breakaway parish in 1889. It was demolished in the 1970s. The trouble with widening roads is that there does seem always to be an increase in traffic. That was fine if other streets can cope. To a point they could. High Street was well able to at that time, but that could not be said about the numerous side streets leading off it, especially round All Saints Church. Part of the Black Boy public house site and the church yard had to be removed to widen the road. Solving one traffic problem created another.

Paul's Row was the town's traditional centre for the trade of cattle and livestock. By 1966 much of Paul's Row was demolished as the new shopping centre came into being. This 1904 photograph shows the laying of the town's main sewer. The machine in the foreground is a pump to keep the trench dry. This was the time when towns were forced to improve the provision for waste disposal and sewerage purification. Diseases such as typhus were rampant at the time. No matter how many improvements were being made or how many fewer people were suffering from diseases, the corporation could not stand still and a public health

system had to be constantly developed. An indication of progress would be the drastic reduction in the number of houses with pail closets; it was about this time that in this part of High Wycombe one outdoor closet was being shared by forty people. There needed also to be public lavatories, an efficient refuse collection and disposal system and a scheme for public education. The problems that confront us today concerning the effects of domestic and industrial waste and the host of other issues which affect people's standard of living have existed for years and will continue to do so.

The traditional method of conveying chairs from the High Street in High Wycombe to London in the late 19th and early 20th centuries was by horse drawn cart either to the railway station or directly by road. The latter would involve a two day journey but then in March 1903 the factory of William Keen in West End Road found that it could save time and carry more chairs with this new fangled steam driven cart, complete with iron-shod wheels. Like all new innovations it certainly drew the crowds not only to admire the well known art of stacking the chairs, but now this mechanical wonder. The William Keen factory had been rebuilt following a fire in 1898 and like many other disasters it had some positive side effects in that it could modernise in more ways than one. From it came more efficiency with the cart bearing twice as many chairs. Travelling at 6mph it could make the return journey in 14 hours. Here was the new factory surely stealing a march on its many rivals in the town. The furniture industry dominated the town for nearly two hundred years and that is remembered in the display at the grand Wycombe Museum which concentrates on the lives of the men and women in the past who worked in the furniture trade like the 'bodgers' to the more modern methods of production.

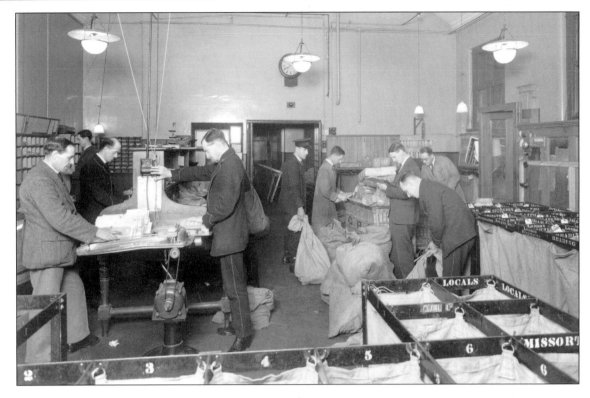

Above: A pre-first world war photograph of a building in Oxford Road. Shades of the economic politics of the time with talk of protectionism, the value of British trade abroad and the threat to it caused by German economic expansion. A feature of the General Election of 1905 was the tariffs that countries like Germany, Canada, France and the United States were putting on imported goods thus making it harder to sell British goods abroad. The 'Free Traders' wanted all import duties to be scrapped. Others wanted Britain to be as protectionist as the Germans. This country feared most of all German military and economic expansion. Considering what was to come those fears were justified. What would also concern the working

man was his livelihood, as British jobs would be threatened - as would trade at home and especially abroad. The populace for the first time began to appreciate the power of their vote. Trade Unions became more effective just as the political and economic power of this country had to face the growing strength of other countries. The message here is simple to understand - protect British interests and British jobs. The debate still continues today.

Top: The Post Office sorting room in the new premises on Queen Victoria Road. A 1930s view of the Post Office workers manually sorting the mail. 'Mis-sorts' sounds as though someone has made a mistake, the sender most likely, not the sorter. This was a new spacious building designed to meet the increased demand for postal and telegraph services. The old Post Office had been situated in Easton Street since 1901 but as the town grew then Easton Street became on the edge of rather than in the centre of the town's business and commercial life. The council acquired valuable land off the High Street and offered an inducement of £1000 to the Postmaster General's Department. The postal authorities refused to move from Easton Street much to the dismay of the Council and the businessmen of the town. The land was bought and there was nothing to build on it. Corporation Street was termed a 'costly white elephant'. Eventually the Post Office move was made to Queen Victoria Road and the grand building compared very favourably with the other buildings there. What a pity that its public functions have been removed. The sorting office has remained but the Post Office has decided that the public is better served in a shopping centre. Understandable, maybe.

Providing more than just a roof

The advent of World War II, brought with it significant changes to the character of High Wycombe. In September 1939, High Wycombe was declared a reception area for evacuees and thousands of mothers, children and teachers poured into the town. Overnight, the population increased by about 3,000 and by 1941 there were an additional 2,000 unaccompanied children, 7,500 mothers and children and 500 War workers with their families.

With peace new industries came into the town and the monopoly held by furniture factories began to diminish.

Housing was in woefully short supply and council house building only provided for people displaced from their older properties in the centre of town, which were being demolished under clearance orders. There was no provision for the new-comers. During the decade which followed the War, only 2,700 homes were built by the local authority.

Above left: *W J Winter Taylor, the first Chairman.*
Right: *Mr and Mrs Munger and family, some of the first tenants of the Association. Three generations of their family have lived in the same cottage at Naphill.* **Below:** *Folly Cottages in the early 1950s.*

Private house building was almost at a standstill due to an acute shortage of building materials and the problems of rationing. In desperation in 1946 squatters not only from the town but also from London took possession of the huts vacated by the American Air Force at Daws Hill.

In response to this acute housing shortage a group of local businessmen and women met at the Friends' Meeting House, London Road, High Wycombe on 18 April 1944 to found the Buckinghamshire Housing Association Ltd. The new association registered as an Industrial and Provident Society, adopted non charitable rules as the founders believed that the landlord tenant contract was an equal relationship and that tenants should not be perceived to be recipients of charity.

3% Loan Stock was issued, redeemable at three months notice at any time after 31st December 1949. BPC was an early shareholder and retained its voting rights until the demise of Robert Maxwell, much to the confusion of the Official receiver appointed to wind up Maxwell's business interests!

Mr A O Errington, the secretary to the Hampshire Rural Cottage Society and committee member of the Wiltshire Cottage Improvement Society became the sponsor and first Secretary of the Association. The

founding Chairman was William J Winter Taylor the father of the present Chairman.

The founders resolved - "To Assist the improvement of housing conditions; To provide well planned homes in both the town and country districts, generally at rentals on a par with those charged by the local authorities and to ensure that where its influence can be of avail, the amenities of the Countryside shall be preserved, as also shall the ancient buildings."

In September 1944 only five months after the original meeting the Association purchased its first properties, seven tenanted cottages at Naphill for £725 with a 3.5% mortgage from the Cooperative Permanent Building Society. Following improvements, the provision of 'Coppers' were let in June 1945 at rents ranging from 5s 9d to 7s 3d!

Today the descendants of two of the original cottagers still live on the row, and the two families, the Mungers and the Wilsons have lived in the cottages for at least three generations.

In October the Association bought 408 houses in Slough at Upton Lea and Manor park for £207,525. Most of the 3 and 4 bedroomed homes had sitting tenants and many of their children and grandchildren still live on the estate today.

In 1945 three brick and flint cottages were purchased in Prestwood. These were already tenanted and in a very poor state of repair. These cottages were eventually demolished in 1985 to make way for eight, 1 and 2 bed flats. Two of the original tenants still live in the flats, which were built in two phases to avoid the need for temporary accommodation.

The purchase of the Speen Cottages in late 1947 marked the first disagreement in the history of the Association. There was a furious argument in Committee over the price, many members felt that £750 for three cottages was

*Above: Folly Cottages today. **Left:** "Grandpa" Pullen, whose ghost is said to haunt Folly Cottages.*
***Below:** Stone Cottage, Loosely Row, bought by the Association in 1954.*

started life, or at one time or other have lived in the cottages, and it is thought that the ghost of one ex-resident Grandpa Pullen, a fierce old man with a white beard returns periodically to haunt the cottages.

When the Association bought the cottages in 1950 they were virtually derelict, Disaster had struck as a result of flooding caused by a combination of a heavy rain causing the ditches on the Common to burst their banks. As the floods subsided an old bottle well was revealed immediately outside the back door of number 1, adding credence to a local story that many years ago a young girl with babe in arms had tragically fallen down the well one foggy evening while looking for her husband who was late home from work,

In 1950 one of the founding members of the Association Miss Mary Towerton donated an acre of land. She is best remembered by those who knew her as a small sturdy figure with a warm smile, bright twinkling eyes and a determined stride which reflected her strong feminist principals and a progressive attitude to life.

The land was used to develop St. Hugh's Close which was completed in late 1952 providing 12 bungalows with common room facilities and was let to professional people in their late 50s and early 60s.

Additional units were added during the early 70s and late 80s and today the scheme comprises 34 dwellings with common room, laundry and guestroom facilities with two wardens providing 24 hour on- call support for the residents.

excessive and to spend a further £750 to provide a new cesspool and piped cold water was downright irresponsible! However the cottages were let in June 1948 at weekly rents of between 12s 0d and 15s 0d.

Aveluy Cottage was named after the 1st World War skirmish at Aveling Wood where the then tenant, Lucy Janes' husband had been killed. Lucy brought up her family at the cottages and died there and her son Les lived on the row for the whole of his life. "Aveling" became Aveluy when a member of the Association's staff misread the name in the deeds.

Five cottages in Lent Rise, Burnham were purchased by the Association in 1948. The cottages date back 300 years, it is thought that number 8 Church walk was originally a farm and number 10 was an attached barn Indeed evidence of the old "salting stone" can still be seen in the living room of No 10.

Another historically interesting set of cottages located on Moor Common outside the picturesque village of Frieth was bought in late 1949 for £250. Folly cottages are a very early example of social housing. In the years between 1845-1855 the Common with its numerous tenanted garden plots became overrun with gypsies and a local landowner, Mr Scott-Morray erected six terraced cottages, to house some of the gypsy families, thus both tidying up the Common and solving the immediate housing needs of the "Travellers". At one time the two-up-two-down cottages boasted of as many as 30 children sleeping approximately five to a bed, situated in the small landing bedrooms. The locals perhaps reflecting the popular Opinion of Mr Scott-Morrays venture christened the cottages The Folly! Over the years many a local family has

Top left: *The 1985 development at Prestwood.*
Right: *Mr Charles Winter Taylor, son of the founder Chairman and Chairman of the Association from 1990 until 1999.*

In 1952 the Association purchased a group of tenanted cottages in Seer Green. It is reputed that in ancient times the village was the regular stopping point of Merlin, on route between London and Camelot, the seer held court on the green by the village well which was situated in Orchard Road, opposite Moss Court. Thus the area became known thereafter as Seer Green.

By 1973 the original sixteenth century cottages were in major disrepair and the association incorporated them into a development of 10 flats with some of the flats boasting inglenook fireplaces and genuine 16th century beams. Over the years another 12 flats have been provided on the site including 4 units purposely designed for wheelchair users.

By 1953 Bucks Housing Association was in financial difficulties due to the rapid expansion programme. A nine-month moritoriam was agreed with the funders to allow the Association breathing space. The Association devised a rescue plan, which involved the sale of some of the Slough properties to the resident tenants and by March 1955 the Association was back on a sound financial footing. Happily by 1958 there were substantial cash surpluses.

However even during these difficult times the Association managed to continue to develop and Stone Cottage, Loosely Row, was bought in late 1954 for £115, and refurbished at a cost of £833 with the help of a Local Authority Grant of £350.

In 1962 William J Winter Taylor resigned as Chairman and was made a life President of the Association. Mrs Mary Towerton took the Chair but unfortunately, due to ill health she was forced to resign in July 1964. Mr Eric Webb briefly became Chairman, and

was succeeded by Mr J H P Roberts in July 1965. He was succeeded by Charles Winter Taylor, the son of the founder, in 1990.

Charles Marcel Winter Taylor was born in High Wycombe at Bassetsbury Manor and was educated locally at the William Borlase School in Marlow. In 1942 he joined the Flight Airarm as a radio mechanic. He was based at Scappa Flow but served in the Mediterranean and the Far East and Australia, where he met his wife Molly. During the early 50s, while temporarily in need of a home they lived for a short time in one of the Association's cottages in Naphill and he still maintains that being a tenant was a good learning experience and provided a valuable alternative perspective in his dealings with tenants.

He qualified as a solicitor in 1950. Although he undertook most of the Association's legal work his father prevented him for many years from becoming actively involved in the management committee as he felt that one Winter Taylor was enough. He finally joined the Management Committee in 1980 becoming Chairman in 1990. Sadly he resigned in September of this year but remains as Vice Chairman providing invaluable help and support to our new Chairman Bryan Rynn.

A plot of land in Geralds Road, High Wycombe was bought in 1965 from the Church Commissioners on a 99-year lease. Church Court, a development of 8 flats was built on the site, these were virtually rebuilt in late 1986 as part of a major refurbishment programme. The association continued to grow during the late 60s and early 70s.

Quarrywood House, Marlow was re-developed to provide four flats and two semi-detached houses. The scheme remains for the most part unchanged, however during the early 1990s, one of the ground floor flats was altered and

Top left: *The opening of New Cottage, Speen.*
Above: *The certificate awarded to the Association for supporting local child victims of crime.* ***Below:*** *Well known children's TV character, Bungle Bear assists in the opening of Briarswood, 1994.*

refurbished vacant properties on assured tenancies outside the Right-to-Buy. The 1968 Housing Act extended this to all re-lets and in early 1990 consent was obtained to transfer to Charitable Rules exempting the Association from Corporation tax and further protecting its housing stock.

The proceeds of the Right to Buy sales generated £1 million in liquid reserves. The money was used to re-improve the housing stock and fund new development. During the late 80s and early 90s over £3.5 million was spent improving our houses and developing new homes.

The Housing Association movement was altering, successive government legislation continually changed the environment in which we worked and in early 1985 the Association appointed its first full time director. In 1987 the Association leased purpose built offices in central High Wycombe and in 1995 it bought the current offices at 86a Easton Street. There is a current staff complement of eight full time and two part time staff, Including the two wardens at St Hugh's Close.

extended to provide accommodation for a family with a severely disabled child who needed the help of a resident carer.

The Old Bakehouse, Stokenchurch was purchased for £5,000 from the local GP's who had used it as a surgery, and converted it into two flats which were let at £6.50 and £8.50 per week.

1975 was a landmark year for the Association as its application for registration with the Housing Corporation was accepted. The Housing Corporation was and continues to be the agency appointed by central government to oversee the work of housing associations and provide grant funding. The Association up dated its Rules to allow it to borrow up to £2,000,000 to fund new developments. The structure was now in place for major expansion, however ambition was tempered with caution based on past experience and in the end the Management Committee decided to only fund new projects from its cash reserves.

The 1980s opened with a challenge to the Association's survival. The Housing Act 1980 promoted the extension of owner occupation, introducing the Right-to-Buy for all tenants of non-charitable housing associations which had received public subsidy. Applications flooded in and by the end of the decade the Association had been forced to sell almost half its housing stock!

Despite the difficulties Bucks HA Ltd was determined to maintain its success and started to investigate ways of protecting its assets. In 1987 the Association was awarded Approved Body status which meant it could let new and

Much has changed since 1944!

The late 70s and early 80s had seen a decline in the development programme but the appointment of a full time Director enabled the Association to restart developing starting with the purchase of the Speen Bakery at 46 High Street, Princes Risborough in early 1985 for £90,000. Numerous unsuccessful attempts were made to get a residential planning permission and at one stage the land was sold for commercial use, however, the purchaser withdrew at the last minute forfeiting his deposit of over £50k. Finally in 1992 suitable planning permission was obtained and the site was developed with the help of Housing Association Grants to provide four units of accommodation for the over 55s including two units especially adapted for wheelchair users.

In the autumn of the same year the Association bought 17 Station Road, Chinnor which was redeveloped to provide two, 1-bed flats and two, 1-bed cottages. These were let in September 1986.

The close of 1985 saw the purchase of a pair of Regency houses in London Road, High Wycombe for £165,000. Initially they were divided into four flats but in 1997 they were converted back into a pair of six bed houses to

Above: *An aerial view of one of the Association's developments, Briarswood at Stokenchurch.*

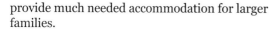

provide much needed accommodation for larger families.

In 1988 the freehold of Russel Court a development of owner occupied sheltered flats for the over 55s was transferred to the Association for just £1!
In 1991 the Association received its first allocation of government funding to develop eight family units on land already owned by the Association in Stokenchurch. This development was completed in May 1994 and opened by the then Housing Minister, Sir George Young.

In 1993 funding was increased to over £900,000 to fund the development of 11 houses in Stokenchurch, 8 flats in High Wycombe and a pair of cottages in Hughenden Valley.

Preservation of the traditional Bucks Cottages was not forgotten and during that year the Association purchased Crown Cottage in Lacey Green at a very reduced price so that it could be let to a villager at an affordable rent. Unfortunately it was not possible to save the original cottage due to structural problems but an exact replica was completed in 1994. At the Wycombe Swan the occasion was marked with a special cake in the shape of a parchment scroll listing the milestones accomplished by the Association during its 50 years of existence.

The Association continued to flourish throughout the 90s and between 1995 and 1999 an additional 88 units of housing have been developed. The redevelopment of the Speen Shop has perhaps had the greatest impact. Prior to the Association purchasing the site in 1995 the shop had been closed for almost 10 years and was virtually derelict. The shop was demolished and replaced with a new village shop and post office and 5 new brick and flint cottages, for rent to local families, were built on the land behind. The houses were part funded by a grant from the Housing Corporation and the National

Lotteries Charitable Board donated £40,000 towards the cost of building the shop. This development has re-vitalised the community and the rental income from the shop is donated back to the village to help fund a variety of projects including a millennium pageant and the restoration of the War Memorial.

The Association's Mission commits us to:

"Providing the highest standard of housing as economically as possible for those in greatest housing need at a rent they can afford".

The Buckinghamshire Housing Association was founded on the principle of mutual respect and from its inception saw its tenants as part of an equal relationship. Tenants remain the first priority. So as we move into the next millennium, it is that mutuality which forms the basis of the "Helping Hand" we offer each other and our determination to provide "more than just a roof !"

Above: The proprietors of the "Useful Little Shop" at Speen. **Top left:** *How the store appeared before refurbishment.* **Below:** *Celebrating the Associations Golden Jubilee in 1995, Charles Winter Taylor, Chairman is pictured with Directors of the Association.*

The company that is forging ahead

Britain's furniture town, has provided over 100 years work for the ironmongery firm, Isaac Lord Ltd. The company has provided both tools and materials for the furniture and woodworking industries in High Wycombe since1892. A feeling of nostalgia is evoked for many people by an ironmongery shop with its distinctive smell. Although there are fewer and fewer left to be found in our towns and cities, Isaac Lord Ltd is one of them and plans to remain so for the next century of successful trade.

Isaac Lord began his working life as a coachman's boy to a doctor in Easton Street, High Wycombe. His ambition did not allow him to stay there long and he soon went on to work at Huntley and Palmer's biscuit factory in Reading where he earned good money enabling him to save for the future. Isaac left this job and returned to Buckinghamshire to marry his childhood sweetheart, Elizabeth. It was then that Isaac made his first connection with the furniture industry working in partnership with Mr. Janes making and selling parts for chairs.

Isaac's ambition led him to branch out on his own. Isaac Lord Ltd, as it is today, began life when on Saturday, 13th February, 1892 Isaac and his wife opened up their shop in the west end of town at 178 Desborough Road. The shop opened at 7 am each day so that workmen could buy their tools on their way to work. The takings on the opening day were a rather disappointing, 3s 9d (20p)! However, as the shop's reputation spread the takings improved and by 1895 Elizabeth was able to record in her accounts book takings of £10 for a week. This success meant that Isaac had to stop working as a benchman with Mr. Janes and that larger premises were needed for his own business. Fortunately, in1901, 202 Desborough Road became available and the Lord's purchased this three storey building for £515.

By 1914 the Lord's had extended their stock to include everything from galvanised baths and buckets, to garden and kitchen tools and had earned itself the reputation as the, 'West End Ironmonger'. However, the advent of the first world war brought with it several changes for the business. Hilda, Isaac and Elizabeth's daughter, gave up her job in Scotland to help her parents in the shop. Their son George also lent a hand in the shop and took over the accounts for his mother. Some chairs were being produced for military use but many of the factories were now

Above left: *Isaac Lord, founder of the company.*
Below: *The Lord family circa 1912. Isaac Lord is third from the left with his wife, Elizabeth on his right.*

producing munition boxes, tent pegs and bomb slings. This meant that woodscrews, nails, sandpaper and glue were needed and Isaac supplied them enabling the business to trade as well as it could with the inevitable shortages experienced during this time.

The end of the war saw George working full time for the business and Isaac and Elizabeth moved from above the shop to a new house at Hughenden Road. It was not however, until the end of 1919 that the business began to recover and in 1921 Isaac handed over the control of the business entirely to Hilda and George. Sadly, only two years later in 1923 Isaac died at the age of 61. The following year saw a recession with serious effects for the furniture industry and in turn a decrease in sales for Isaac Lord. In 1918 cash sales had amounted to £1300 and trade sales to £475. By 1926 however, helped by a boom in house building, the cash sales had grown to £4300 and the trade sales to £6200 and the business was back on track once again. Indeed, by 1925 the business had grown sufficiently to provide a living for another child of Isaac and Elizabeth's,

Dennis who joined the partnership of the firm with George and Hilda.

Despite being in the depths of the world slump in 1931, George managed to purchase an ironmongery business in Station Road, Gerrards Cross, with his brother Ernest. A limited company was formed, 'Lord Bros Ltd', and this shop worked independently from the shop at Desborough Road which had a different variety of stock. The Desborough Road shop was not ignored and in 1932 it was refurbished inside and out making it the first modern shop front in the road. Only two years later a two-storey warehouse with an adjoining house in Richardson Street was purchased This provided the company with the opportunity to expand the pottery, china and glassware sideline of the business and the upper floor of the store was given over entirely to the storage of earthenware and glassware. In 1937, George and Dennis bought the ironmongery business of Benoy and Burnett in Priory Road and employed Walter Webb to run the shop. George's son Horace joined the family firm and worked under Walter learning the trade until the shop was closed in 1958. The final expansion in the inter-war years was the renting of the shop next to the premises in Desborough Road by which time the firm employed 20 people.

The advent of the second world war brought with it restrictions of supplies. Certificates were required from the Ministry of Supply for the purchase of essential materials. This scarcity of goods proved to be an advantage for the firm's sales figures as queues formed outside the shops whenever, for instance, a consignment of saucepans or teapots arrived. In 1943, the company

Above left: *The company's first car. Hilda is at the wheel with Elizabeth beside her. Circa 1922.*
Top: *Isaac with his eldest son, George, circa 1910.*

even managed to purchase another property. Dennis then became a special policeman as well as being appointed to the Board of Trade Committee and the British Standards Committee for Utility Furniture whilst Horace became a member of the Home Guard.

By 1948, over fifty years after its establishment, the original business had expanded enough to become a limited company with George, Dennis and Horace becoming the first Directors. A year later Dennis set up his own ironmongery business in Henley on Thames with his son John. This brought the number of shops displaying the Lord name up to four. These local shops were able to fend off the London competition by providing a unique on-the-spot, off-the-shelf service.

The 1950s were more prosperous years for the country and for the ironmongery trade. The plastic revolution meant that plastic products filled the shelves of the ironmongery shops making them more colourful. Indeed, 'The National Federation of Ironmongers' changed its name to 'The national Hardware Federation' to match this trend. The sale of hand tools declined during these years but luckily wood-turning and wood-carving was a popular hobby and helped to replace this declining market. Another of George's sons, Donald had joined the family business in 1947 and in 1954 Donald opened up a shop in Oxford, 'Lord's of Cowley' extending the Lord ironmongery empire!

During the 1960s the retail sales at Lord's were dominated by paraffin which was used in almost every home before the invention of central heating. The oil delivery round conducted by the business for years continued also delivering paraffin. This job was more risky than it sounded, especially when one memorable delivery day the truck carrying the paraffin caught fire and exploded like a bomb. Luckily the delivery man was not in the van at the time and nobody was hurt! More sedate products on sale at this time were lawnmowers and Black and Decker tools. Sales of these products were successful with one exception. The company exhibited the new Black and Decker egg cleaning accessory at the Wycombe Show but unfortunately caused more amusement than sales after managing to break most of the eggs!

In 1963, to cope with complaints about the slow counter service in the shop, Lord's opened a new building near Desborough Road with a spacious showroom, offices, a trade counter and store room. This meant that the shop at Desborough Road could now be modernised. Indeed, by 1965 when Horace went to the 'International Exhibition for Suppliers to the Furniture and Woodworking Industries' in Germany, the business was thriving and even found new markets in Europe and

Above left: *An early advertisement.*
Top: *The shop in 1932.*

America. This same year the fourth generation of Lord's joined the family business. Alan, Horace's son worked in the shop at first and after a short spell working for Power Tools Specialists Ltd, came back to the trade department and took responsibility for the sales of power tools.

In the early 1970s the Council decided to widen Desborough Road and the old shop had to be demolished. However, a new larger corner shop was opened on the opposite side of the widened road under the name, 'Lord's Hardware Centre'. Capitalising on the popularity of DIY, the firm's first trade catalogue was produced and within two years of the move sales had increased by 50%! In 1977 the company accounts system was computerised and this, as well as its lower prices, enabled Lord's to compete with the DIY superstores. The old adage, 'You will probably get it at Lord's' was still used when talking of the modern shop.

When Horace retired in 1985 David and Alan united the wholesale and retail sections of the business and shared control as managing directors of the four sales departments: warehouse; power tools; hand tools; and shop. A

new building was purchased on Desborough Industrial Park to store all the trade stock allowing the shop to be refurbished and extended. The shop was officially opened by the boxer Henry Cooper in 1987 and soon after tool sales improved.

Isaac Lord Ltd celebrated its centenary year in 1992 and seven years later a new trade counter and warehouse was opened in Bristol. Over 100 years later Isaac and Elizabeth would be amazed to see the new Lord buildings however, they would probably still recognise Desborough Road and indeed, would recognise the tradition of friendly, helpful and efficient service that they first established in 1892.

Above: *The company display at an ASFI Exhibition at the NEC in the late 1980s.*
Left: *Isaac Lord FC in 1980.* **Below:** *The Desborough Road premises in the late 1990s.*

Craftsmanship and technology - a perfect combination

The Ercol Furniture Limited Company came into existence in the year 1920 when it was founded by Lucian R Ercolani, later known as Lucian R Ercolani OBE FRSA. The history of this now internationally successful business can however, be traced as far back as the 19th century.

It was at the turn of this century that the Ercolani family made the decision to emigrate from their home in Italy. In the year 1888 the young Lucian R Ercolani, accompanied by his family, made the important journey all the way from Florence in Italy to his new home in England. This was an exciting event for Lucian, filled with opportunity. At only 14 years of age the young Italian had already determined on a career in some kind of artistic pursuit. Lucian, intent on not wasting any time, made the first step towards fulfilling his ambition. He sought education through art and to this aim enrolled in a night school at Shoreditch. Lucian attended this school, which was later known as the London College, for many years and built up experience which was to prove invaluable in his future career. By the year 1911 Lucian had honed his ambitious sights to focus specifically on a career in furniture design. It was in this year that, to this end, he signed up for a course in Furniture Design and English

Furniture History. This course was run by the High Wycombe Technical College which was the forerunner of what was to become the Buckinghamshire College of Higher Education. Lucian excelled in his chosen subject and received a City and Guilds Award in Cabinet Making. Indeed, his work was noticed and highly praised by the Cabinet Maker. A particular piece of work that received special attention for its excellence was a beautiful music cabinet which in fact, is still on display at the company to this day.

This acclaim, in the early years of Lucian's career, must have gone some way to securing him the jobs he gained. Indeed, for some years he managed to work at several of High Wycombe's established furniture manufacturers after receiving his City and Guilds Award. In doing so, he gathered more extremely valuable experience - this time of a practical nature. Lucian's next accomplishment was to be offered the post of Lecturer in Furniture Design at Buckinghamshire College the establishment where he had received his training. Lucian did not by any means rest on his laurels and whilst teaching in the evenings he set to work as a Commercial Designer

Below: *Chairmaking in the early days.*

during the daytime. Initially he worked for Frederick Parker at Parker-Knoll and then later, for Ebenezer Gomme at G-Plan.

Lucian R Ercolani had then, throughout the initial stages of his career and education built up an extensive and comprehensive background of practical experience and technical expertise. By the year 1920, the innovative Lucian's entrepreneurial spirit was eager for a new challenge and so, to this aim, he founded his own

company, Ercol Furniture Limited. The company was set up on the basis of Lucian's philosophy, which was one of developing skills and craftsmanship through a consuming love of design and quality - a philosophy still upheld by the company today. The company was established and located at London Road in High Wycombe. Indeed, Ercol Furniture Limited has remained on this site ever since its foundation making it a truly local firm.

The burgeoning company began to flourish and prosper and became increasingly successful in the years preceding the second world war. However, the advent of the second world war brought with it several extensive changes to the workings of Ercol Furniture Limited. During the war years the design and production of furniture was brought to a stand still. The company was converted entirely over to war work and played an important role in the war effort. Numerous essential wood work products were manufactured at the firm including items from life saving rafts to tent pegs and ammunition boxes.

Top: *Lucian R Ercolani, ('The Old Man'), and his sons Lucian, (extreme left of the picture) and Barry (middle of the picture) seen in discussion in the Board Room in 1962.* ***Above left:*** *Edward Tadros (present Chairman and Managing Director, and grandson of the founder) with colleague.*

The cessation of the second world war saw Ercol Furniture Limited managing to get successfully back on track reaching the thriving heights of the pre-war years. After the war a new and far better educated public began to emerge and Lucian set out to achieve an individuality of design and construction which in turn created a style unique to Ercol Furniture Limited. He also began to use methods and techniques that would encourage other manufacturers to copy and follow by his example.

Immediately after the war Lucian installed yet another change within his company. This change however, was of a social nature. Lucian bought up all the instruments form the local Home Guard and enlisted anyone in the company who could blow or play an instrument. This enlistment brought about the establishment of the Ercol Band. At first, after many hours of practice, the band began by playing to factory employees once or twice a week and this soon developed into popular performances at local fetes.

Top: *Renaissance and Cloister frames being made in 1994.* **Above right:** *The Ercol band playing at the ceremony of the lighting up of the Norwegian Christmas Tree.*

Lucian R Ercolani had already achieved his boyhood ambition to design and build his own furniture and to establish his own successful company. However, even his childhood ambitions were surpassed when in the years following the war his two sons, Lucian and Barry Ercolani, joined their father in his business. Ercol Furniture Limited could now boast the status of a family business and indeed, it has retained this family orientation ever since. Lucian Junior had, like

Ercol Furniture Limited made another breakthrough in its history when it managed to tame Elm. The company devised unique techniques to stabilise and control the fickle wood and a steady stream of furniture craftsmen and research bodies have visited the company ever since to learn about these pioneering methods. In about 1985 Ash became the company's third timber alongside Beech and Elm. Indeed, the company controls its own supply of the woods and employs a specialist to hand pick the trees. Ercol now has its own sawmills and wood yards in the States enabling it to provide the highest quality furniture.

Today, Ercol Furniture Limited has grown into an internationally successful company exporting goods as far afield as Japan, Australia, the Middle East and North America. The company has been awarded over 26 Design Craft Guild Marks by The Worshipful Company of Furniture Makers of the City of London. It has also played its part in the local community through education and sponsorship. In fact, in 1999 the company planted 400 broad leafed trees at Keep Hill which can be seen across the valley from the Ercol factory site. Edward Tadros is the present Managing Director of the business and grandson of the founder. Thus, ensuring that the company continues to function as a family concern maintaining its status amongst the top ten furniture manufacturers in Britain and the largest manufacturer of solid wood furniture.

Top left: *One of the most successful products made by Ercol in recent years, the Renaissance collection.*
Below: *Edward Tadros, with one of the famous Swan chairs.*

his father, shown a specific talent from an early age ever since his shoolboy years. Lucian Junior's particular flair was however, for mechanical engineering and application. Indeed, he worked hard and soon matured into a Machine Designer for the company. In this role he also played a significant part in bringing about an extension of furniture design to incorporate the means to create specialised devices and machinery. Lucian R Ercolani's younger son, Barry, also had the determination and ambition shown by his father. Barry's first allocated task in the family business was that of looking after sales immediately after the war. He fulfilled this role admirably and vowed that he was going to assist the company in getting the recognition it seemed to deserve. Indeed, in his time at the firm he accomplished this task and not only spread the message throughout this country but also to many other countries around the world.

As a family concern, the business continued to thrive and develop. In 1947 they astonished the furniture world by making a Windsor Chair entirely by mechanised means. This was a considerable breakthrough since the Windsor Chair had been arduously made by hand in the area for centuries. Ercol always remained at the forefront of technology, assisted by the most sophisticated machinery and computers. Indeed, the outstanding achievement in this case was not the rate of production but the fact that the new methods had established standards far above those of previous manual methods. The extent of the accomplishment in producing the chair can be seen in its standing as the best selling Windsor Chair in the United Kingdom, even today. The company's band also achieved its own success. In 1977 the band played at the Silver Jubilee in Hyde Park and a year later it played Christmas carols at the lighting of the Norwegian Christmas Tree in Trafalgar Square - a tradition which it has upheld ever since.

At the cutting edge of service

The company now known as Southern Counties Saws has a history reaching back over more than 75 years. The company first started life in 1923, trading under the name, H Pickles and Son (Saws) Limited. The name H Pickles, in the company's title, was taken from its founder, Harry Pickles.

Harry Pickles spent the first part of his working life employed in a totally different type of pursuit to the manufacture of saws. He was in fact, a horse breeder. Quite what led Harry from horse breeding to setting up his own saw manufacturing business will never be fully known, but make this extraordinary transition he did! In 1923 H Pickles and Son (Saws) Limited was established. Harry was joined by his son in their new venture and they set to work with the business of manufacturing and servicing all types of saws.
Harry and his son based their new business at premises located in Dashwood

Avenue, High Wycombe. Indeed, this was to prove to be a perfect choice of location and the company remained at this first base for a total of 71 years until 1994 whereupon the firm relocated to new premises at Lincoln Road on Cressex Business Park. Although H Pickles and Son (Saws) Limited manufactured all types of saws, Harry and his son found themselves mainly producing and servicing the wide band type of saw. H Pickles used quality carbon steel as their main material and this is another aspect of the company that remains unchanged even today.

H Pickles and Sons (Saws) Limited, developed the business successfully, giving it a flourishing start. The company's saws were advertised under the name, Planet Saws and the catch-phrase, 'For all Round Good Service' circled a picture of the planet earth in the company's promotional posters! It was not long before Pickles and Sons' fine, well made saws established an excellent wide reaching reputation. Indeed, the company began to gain a world wide reputation and was able to start exporting its goods. Pickles and Sons goods

Right: *An early advertising brochure, dated 1937.*
Below: *The workshop pictured in 1940.*

enormous value to the West African territories with their development schemes'. Naturally then, one of the first class companies represented by Glyndova was Hodges and Pickles. The company had carried out a great deal of research in connection with the cutting of West African Hardwoods and this research had produced the so called, 'Super Planet' bronze finish band saw. The company also provided a 'School for Saw Doctors' which could be used by overseas operators to train men for their African staff. Indeed, both these assets were represented by Glyndova in West Africa to successful ends.

The advent of the second world war brought with it a troublesome period for the company. At this time it was extremely difficult to acquire the correct steel needed to manufacture the saws to the company's usual high standards. The company had to endure a period of slow trade and a halt to further development and continued growth.

were exported to many different countries. Initially, India and Pakistan received the majority of the exports however, by the time the company was known by the name, Hodges and Pickles, the exports were reaching West Africa.

The company was represented in West Africa by Glyndova. Glyndova had offices in Nigeria and the Gold Coast and specialised in representing British firms in these countries. Glyndova prided itself on only representing 'first class' companies with 'British Made', goods with high standards of workmanship. In doing so it believed that it was bringing 'experience and skill of

The company did manage to survive the war years and by 1950 was already undergoing more changes. It was in this year that Harry Pickles was taken over. Southern

Above: *Mr Glendova, far left, with trainees.*
Top: *Robby Robbins teaching trainees the skills for Wide Bandsaw Brazing.*

High Wycombe. Southern Counties Saw Company Limited had been heavily dependent on the furniture industry and had to adapt and change once again in order to survive. With considerable foresight and innovation the company rapidly diversified into other fields. The main areas of diversification were the manufacture of: surgical saws for use in bone grafts and plaster cast cutting, joint replacements and autopsy work; UPVC windows; special saws for the food industry used for cutting meat and fish; and diamond plated saws for the automotive industry.

By 1988 the company was taken over once again, this time by Alan Mawby. Alan had joined the company in 1960 after serving his apprenticeship with High Wycombe Saw Mill and worked his way through the company until he could finally afford to buy it!

Today, the company continues to be successful and its main markets remain to be the medical, furniture and food industries. Although the company has seen many changes throughout its history, as it moves towards its centenary year it continues to manufacture products literally at the cutting edge!

Counties was one of the companies that took control of the business, the other was, South Midland. The three companies were amalgamated and the new, expanded company operated under the name Southern Counties Saw Company Limited which incorporated South Midland Saws Limited and H Pickles Saws Limited. The new company was now run by Roy Styles and Ray Fullick and it has been trading under the name, Southern Counties Limited ever since this amalgamation.

The owner of the newly named company had been associated with the original company before the war and was trained by the old Sheffield craftsmen in saw smithing and the specialist skills needed to satisfy the requirements of the many different trades using saws at that time. The advent of plastics and many other man-made materials brought new challenges to the business. Further skills were needed to keep up with the demands of the new materials and it was necessary to build a team to supply this expertise.

A specialist team was built up and this later helped to gain the company the distinction of becoming one of the leaders in tungsten carbide products, offering a wide range of circular, TCT and plate saws. The company also had, by then, a comprehensive knowledge of manufacturing, maintenance and re-tipping, all of which provided cost-cutting services for the many industries with which it was involved. The log cutting and narrow bandsaw manufacture and repair department had also established a wide knowledge which was of great value to the company's increasing customer base which now included: Ghana; Nigeria; America; Canada; Austria; Germany; New Zealand; and Australia. Indeed, all these factors helped the company to continue to thrive.

The 1980s brought with them a decline in the furniture trade of

Above: Staff at a Christmas party in 1962.
Below: Just a few of the saws that the company produces. Bottom: The company in the 1990s.

Providing the antiques of tomorrow

The Bartlett family has been producing traditional furniture for over 120 years. The business started life in 1864 when its founder, William Bartlett began making Windsor Chairs in partnership with one of his friends.

The pair made the chairs by hand, buying the legs and other turned parts from country 'Bodgers' in the Buckinghamshire Beech woods and the seats, tops and uprights from local sawmills. The partners sold their chairs for only 24 shillings a dozen, including delivery! However, from these humble beginnings the business grew and when the partnership dissolved, William moved to progressively larger premises.

During the late 1890's William branched out and began making cabinet goods. This proved to be a wise decision and the business began to flourish. By 1901, William was able to purchase a four and a half acre factory site which the company still uses today!

The advent of the first world war brought with it many difficulties but the business managed to survive. Indeed, in 1918 a partnership between William and his son George was incorporated in order to form a limited liability company. The business was carried on by two of George's sons and subsequently, his grandson making it truly, a family concern.

Another landmark decision was made by the company in 1959. It was resolved to concentrate production on furniture based on traditional design, of which the company was a pioneer in the pre 1914 era. Indeed, to this day it remains a leading manufacturer of this style of furniture.

Today, aided by a workforce of 130 people, the company continues to thrive. The company now designs and constructs the Strongbow Mahogany and Yew furniture ranges. This furniture brings the elegance

Top left: *William Bartlett, who founded the firm in 1864.*
Right, both pictures: *Just two examples of the ranges of furniture produced by William Bartlett.*

of 'The Golden Age of English Furniture' from the 18th century and Regency periods to the 20th century household. This, together with modern manufacturing techniques ensure the long life of the furniture. Today, many Computer Numerical Control machines are in operation however, in some cases the old machines are still the best. Indeed, the 48" bandsaws, made for the company in 1911, are irreplaceable for chair making! Skilled craftsmen also remain vital in the production of the furniture and the company has its own training programme to ensure these skills are maintained.

William Bartlett and Son Ltd is still a family concern and two great grandsons of the founder, William, currently work for the company. With the introduction of a new logo; a new web site; refurbished showrooms; and a new range of Cherry furniture, William Bartlett intend to continue making the antiques of the future well into the foreseeable future!

A place in which there is a true love of learning

In the tranquil setting of the Chilterns countryside in Great Kingshill a tablet erected in 1999 on a newly landscaped memorial terrace testifies to the debt of gratitude owed to a remarkable lady: Miss Jessie Cross. It was her vision that created the school which has become Pipers Corner and her spirit which lives on in this thriving community.

The school was originally established in Richmond in 1930 as "The Old Vicarage School" but most pupils moved out of London during the Blitz to Prestwood Lodge in Nairdwood Lane. Miss Cross rented the Lodge on a monthly basis and for a time ran both schools, using her petrol rations to commute from Buckinghamshire to Richmond each week, often ferrying baskets of the boarders' laundry.

The regime of the wartime years was very different from today's routines. Parents were asked to bring beds (as well as bed linen); the Headmistress kept pigs and the gardener grew adequate supplies of fruit and

Above: Miss Jessie Cross who founded the school in 1930. Below: An aerial view of the school and its peaceful rural surroundings.

vegetables to ensure that the girls never went hungry. The day began with two brisk circuits of the walled garden and house before breakfast, and, on Sundays, ended with the National Anthems of the Allies, all girls standing up for "God Save the King". For a while, the pupils had to do "war work": gardening, saving logs, collecting scraps from the village for the pigs.

The range of the curriculum was sometimes restricted owing to the difficulties of obtaining teaching staff during the war. However, in addition to English, Mathematics, French, Biology, History, Geography, Religious Knowledge, Art, Singing and Games, the girls enjoyed a session of Eurhythmics every Monday afternoon. To take their School Certificate, girls travelled to the Royal Masonic School in Rickmansworth.

The present day and boarding school, now a registered Charity, came into being with the purchase of the Pipers Corner property at the end of Pipers Lane in July 1945. The school was officially opened by the Bishop of Buckingham on 23rd March 1946 and soon after there followed recognition from the Ministry of Education. At this time, there were about one hundred pupils, half boarders and half day girls.

Development continued apace. 1956 saw the construction of the Dining Room, Chapel and the (then) New Pool; later additions were a new office and kitchen extension, a new Library, new dormitories, a music room and extra classroom accommodation.

Five heads have guided the progress of the school since its beginnings but the essential ethos has remained the same. Successive generations of Pipers girls and staff have acknowledged their good fortune in growing and working in the idyllic surroundings of the 36 acre grounds.

Many have recently returned to renew their acquaintance with their "Alma Mater" since the relaunch of the Old Girls' Association under the inspired name of "Cornerstones"

The girls at Pipers today pursue a very varied programme both inside and outside the classroom. Fundamental to the school's philosophy is the conviction that every girl has ability, whether it be in the academic sphere, in music, drama, art, public speaking, debating or on the games field. To that extent, there is definitely no such thing as a "Pipers girl" stereotype for all are confident and well-rounded young people.

A list of all development projects in the final decade of the millennium would be a lengthy chronicle. An indoor swimming pool and fitness centre is under construction on the site of the old orchard. This facility will complement the existing Sports Hall built in 1990. The premises of the Pre-Preparatory Department for girls aged between 4 and 7 which were opened as recently as 1994 are shortly to be extended. Girls at the other end of the age range are housed in the Spinney which was converted for Sixth Form use in 1990. Five years later, the Cottesloe Centre, named after Lord Cottesloe, then Lord Lieutenant for Buckinghamshire, became the focus of the Performing Arts and Technology facilities.

A statue, donated by the sculptress Rachel Landau (who is remembered in the assembly hall which bears her name) has become a centrepiece of the new atrium Reception and smiles benignly on all visitors to the school. If, like Pygmalion's statue, she had the gift of speech, she might greet visitors with the words of Jessie Cross to:

"a place in which there is a true love of learning, where there is a commitment not only to academic achievement but also to the development of each girl as a whole person with a very real sense of social and moral responsibility."

Above: The main school building.
Right: The highly successful Public Speaking Team.

Providing a helping hand

The distressed and sick residents of High Wycombe have been receiving help and care in the town at least since the building of the town's oldest hospital before the granting of Wycombe's Charter. This help continued during the following years via churches and individuals. Indeed, an important source of help in the town came from the Royal Grammar School. The school made various charitable provisions such as the Almshouses and also set up several funds. Amongst these were the Samaritan Fund and the Sick Poor Fund.

These two funds became the basis of the Central Aid Society. Frances Dove (later Dame Frances) was the formidable headmistress of Wycombe Abbey School and the first female Councillor of the Borough of Chepping Wycombe. Every day Frances was faced with people begging at the school gates. This sight compelled her to found the High Wycombe Central Aid Society. The charity was established and registered in 1906 and it began work straight away by administering the Samaritan and the Sick Poor Funds.
The charity was based at the Old Courthouse on

Above: *Frances Dove (later Dame Frances), headmistress of Wycombe Abbey School, who founded the High Wycombe Central Aid Society to help the people she faced begging at the school gates.*

Amersham Hill and was supported by subscriptions from companies and the more well-to-do of the town. Local factory owners, professional people and representatives of similar agencies became trustees of the charity and had overall responsibility for the work and decisions made by the Society. However, the day to day running of the Society was the responsibility of the Secretary assisted by volunteers. Money, food and goods as well as help with travel to hospital was provided by the Society to many needy recipients.

Sadly in 1934, Dame Frances died but the Society's work continued. In 1938 it had become the local arm of SSAFA, Forces Help and a year later the Society embraced the Citizen's Advice Bureau which was part of the Society until 1971 when it became independent in order to expand its staff and services. In 1944, an initiative brought the British Red Cross and the Women's Voluntary Service together and in doing so laid the basis for the Society's Medical Loan Facility with which the Society was associated until 1998.

After the cessation of the second world war several Old People's Clubs were established, many of which are still flourishing today. From the establishment of these clubs it was a natural progression to become responsible for the Old People's Welfare which later became Age Concern, High Wycombe and still functions as an integral member of the Society being run from shared offices with SSAFA at the Cornmarket. Other effects of the war, rationing and hardship, caused a rapid increase in the number of people seeking help from the Society and the charity continued with its important work in the town.

Today, the Central Aid Society still continues to survive through the donation of money, food and goods from local people and local businesses. Cases of hardship are referred to the Society from a wide variety of sources and after investigation, action is authorised by the Trustees who meet once a month. Assistance with debts, food, purchase of clothing and medical needs is provided by the Society. The charity also runs a second hand furniture project and clothes store. The furniture is stored in a warehouse in Desborough Road which was formerly the Grand Cinema and volunteers collect items and drop them off to those in need with the help of its van. The Central Aid Society also keeps current information and Fact Sheets on benefits and services for Pensioners and there is a local visiting scheme run by Age Concern,

> *Money, food and goods as well as help with travel to hospital was provided by the Society to many needy recipients*

Buckinghamshire. The Society organises a Pensioners' Pop-In Reggie Goves Centre from St Mary Street which amongst other activities holds Tea Dances and Bingo sessions as well as several different outings. The Forces Help branch of the Society is now administered from the office and includes casework for the Armed Forces Benevolent Funds for serving and ex-service people and dependants.

The Society's work remains substantially the same as it was in 1906, however, the funds needed are much greater. In the 1960's SSAFA cases cost a maximum of £8, whereas an average case today could cost £150! Despite the constant struggle to gather adequate funds, the High Wycombe Central Aid Society manages to continue, in its original aim, of extending a helping hand to, and by caring for the people of High Wycombe in their time of need. Become a Society 'friend' for £5 per year. Tel: 01494 535890.

Below: *Elderly people enjoying a Christmas meal provided by the Old People's Welfare.*

Acknowledgments

High Wycombe Reference Library
Martin Rickard
Steve Cohen, Editor, Bucks Free Press
Mr and Mrs J Gore

Thanks are also due to Kevin McIlroy who penned the editorial text
and Ann Ramsdale for her copywriting skills

87/88 contents

C000185721

Design and production by Trinity Mirror Sport Media

Executive Editor: Ken Rogers • Senior Editor: Steve Hanrahan • Senior Art Editor: Rick Cooke • Senior Production Editor: Paul Dove
Written by: Chris McLoughlin, Chris Brereton • Designed by: Colin Sumpter, Glen Hind & Alison Barkley • Production by: Roy Gilfoyle
Photography: Liverpool Post and Echo archive, Mirrorpix, David McBride (supplied every home & away programme)
© Published in Great Britain in 2013 by Trinity Mirror Sport Media, PO Box 48, Old Hall Street, Liverpool, L69 3EB.

Printed by Buxton Press

CHRIS McLOUGHLIN
KOP MAGAZINE EDITOR

ONLY when you properly experience the bad times do you truly appreciate the good.

As an Anfield regular for 26 years, that phrase has grown more prominent in my mind with every season that passes without Liverpool Football Club winning the league title.

There are days when I wish I'd been born in 1957. To have been a kid at Anfield in the 1960s when Bill Shankly harnessed the power of the Kop and delivered promotion, the championship and that first FA Cup in the space of four glorious seasons.

To have followed Liverpool across Europe as a teen in the 1970s as Bob Paisley took our club's success to unparalleled levels.

But I missed all that. I arrived in this world five months after the glory of Rome and grew up in the 1980s. For that, I count my blessings.

BEST CHRISTMAS GIFT EVER

Christmas Day, 1986. Probably about 5am. Or earlier. Me and our kid were ripping into the presents good old Santa only finished wrapping at about 3am. Or later.

It's funny how you remember certain Christmases as a kid for particular presents you got. 1986 was one of those Christmases. It was boss.

I'd never been to Anfield at that point. Like most families on Merseyside, ours was split over football. My granddad was a red, but my dad was a blue, hence a battle for my allegiances.

Bruce Grobbelaar swung it in Liverpool's favour. I loved his eccentric behaviour and the way he'd rush out of his goal, even if it was often catastrophic with his cock-up for Imre Varadi's goal for Sheffield Wednesday at Anfield in September 1984 my first real memory of a Liverpool game.

From then on, I wanted to be him so Brucie became my first hero and, thankfully, Liverpool became my team. There but for the grace of God and all that.

By the time I was nine, getting to see the Reds at Anfield had become the be-all and end-all. On Christmas Day 1986, Santa Claus obliged. I don't think I've ever seen anything

better in a stocking than tickets for Liverpool versus Newcastle United. Not even in FHM.

We went to the game on January 24. Paul Walsh and Ian Rush netted in a 2-0 win and I was well and truly addicted. Being there was better than I'd even imagined and my mission in life became to keep going again and again and again. And play for the school footie team, obviously.

It means that 1987 will always be a special year for me. It was the year I started going to Anfield to watch Kenny Dalglish's Liverpool and that's why I consider myself lucky to be a child of the late '70s.

I went to a few games in the second half of that 1986/87 season – including the snowy afternoon when Luton actually turned up – but my first full season as a match-going Liverpool supporter was 1987/88.

How good was that? It gives me goosebumps just thinking about it now.

ANXIOUS WAIT FOR NEW ERA

In my mind, the summer of 1987 was baking hot.

Every Liverpool game in the first half of that season seemed to be played in glorious sunshine yet, according to the Met Office, 2012 was the dullest summer since 1987 when the UK saw only 402 hours of sun.

Maybe it's the glorious football Liverpool played that just makes it feel like it was sunnier now.

As a kid, I was desperate for the season to start, but older Reds had a hint of uncertainty about the new campaign.

MAGIC MOMENT: Chris gets an autograph from his hero Bruce Grobbelaar on an unforgettable visit to Anfield

ANXIETY IN THE PIPELINE: A collapsed sewer below the Kop meant the Reds had to wait until September to see their side play at home

BENEATH THE KOP: Work went on underneath the famous terrace so the fans could see their new side against Oxford

Liverpool won nothing in 1986/87. Everton were champions and their biggest nemesis, Ian Rush, had signed for Juventus. Replacing a striker who'd netted 167 goals in six seasons seemed impossible. It wasn't the only concern.

Rushie's chief creator, player-manager Kenny Dalglish, had decided at the age of 36 to pick himself far less and after two years of Bob Paisley working with him as a managerial adviser, he was now leading the team without him.

John Aldridge, Rush's replacement, had arrived in the January, but had only made two starts. He'd scored in both, but even so, how would Liverpool get the best out of him?

John Barnes was signed, but his arrival from Watford was anything but straight-forward.

Publicly admitting he wanted to move abroad and only completing a move to Anfield when no foreign club offered the £900,000 that Liverpool put on the table didn't create a great impression on Merseyside. He had some winning over to do.

Peter Beardsley followed for a club record £1.9 million, effectively as Kenny's replacement. His arrival did set pulses racing (although maybe not with the ladies), but by then there had been another shock to contend with. The Spion Kop was going down the pan. Almost quite literally.

Work to upgrade some of the Kop's crush barriers had been taking place in the first week of July when a giant hole measuring 20ft by 15ft appeared on football's most famous terrace.

A Victorian sewer, built in 1860, had collapsed underneath

the Kop causing a shaft to come crashing down. It would take up to two months to repair, leaving Liverpool with a quandary.

Should they play at Anfield in front of a reduced capacity? Or start the season with three away games? With revenue through the turnstiles being the club's biggest source of income, waiting until September for a home game was risking a cash-flow problem, but that's what the board chose to do.

It meant that the new-look Reds had to postpone home games against Charlton, Derby and Watford with Oxford United's visit to Merseyside on September 12 being the first Anfield fixture.

By the time it came around, excitement and anticipation levels had rocketed. Rarely has the first home game of the season been looked forward to as much.

A BRAND OF FOOTBALL WORTH WAITING FOR

It doesn't matter how old you are. It doesn't matter how many times you've been there. It doesn't even matter who Liverpool are playing.

The buzz that you get from stepping inside Anfield for the first time in a new season never dissipates. It's the adrenalin shot that is impossible to replicate. The energy boost Red Bull can't can. The spring in your step that requires no trainers with air.

That first glimpse of the green grass – and it's always greener when you haven't seen it since May – as you emerge from the concourse towards the sunlight is Anfield's cleavage. A little hint of beauty that instantly makes you long to embrace it.

And as you take to your speck, seeing faces familiar and new, the incomparable sense of belonging that keeps you coming back time and time again surges through your veins. This is Anfield.

You could've multiplied that feeling by 10 back in September '87.

It took precisely nine minutes of Liverpool's opening game of the season down at Highbury to blow away any fears about our team in the post-Rush era.

Dressed in their brand new silver-grey away strip – which I absolutely loved but others hated – Kenny's new-look attacking trio tore the Arsenal defence to shreds.

Beardsley slipped the ball to Barnes on the left and his first-time cross was glanced into the far corner by Aldridge. It was slick, it was stylish and if you weren't at Highbury you had to watch the news that night to see the goals.

KEY SIGNINGS: Kenny captured John Barnes, Peter Beardsley and John Aldridge

As incomprehensible as it now seems, there was no football highlights show every Saturday night at the time. Indeed, live football was also a rarity with the Reds' 4-1 win at Newcastle on September 20 the first Division One game screened live on TV that season.

Both BBC and ITV had the rights back then – you'd get to see a goals round-up on Grandstand and Saint & Greavsie the following weekend – but on weekends when they didn't bother showing highlights (on the weekend of the Oxford game BBC1 screened Miami Vice and ITV had the Dame Edna Experience on instead) you were relying on the Saturday night news bulletin to see a few goals from the day's big games.

That lack of television coverage only added to the anticipation and expectation ahead of Liverpool's first home game. Appetites were well and truly whetted.

After winning 2-1 at Arsenal, they ripped into FA Cup winners Coventry City at Highfield Road the following weekend, hammering them 4-1, before drawing 1-1 at West Ham in a game Liverpool dominated. Even so, the papers were full of hype about the brand of football Kenny's side were playing.

"The fans who pack Anfield tomorrow will soon see the benefits of a more expansive policy, which has enabled the side to attack from at least three different positions rather than funnelling everything through one man," wrote Ian Hargraves in the Liverpool ECHO.

"The accent is now on quickness of movement, with the ball switched from player to player with bewildering rapidity rather than long, measured passes.

"Mobility is certainly the name of the game. The fans are going to enjoy the new style."

I can't remember now, but the chances are I didn't sleep that night. We had tickets for the Oxford game in the Annie Road end which then, don't forget, had brightly coloured orange, purple, white, yellow and green seats.

Down at the Kop end, it cost something like £3 to get in and the queues started that morning.

Liverpool had announced record season ticket sales and the fear of being locked out meant many a Kopite spent their Saturday mornings queueing down Walton Breck Road.

It was a wise move. Hundreds failed to get in and missed some mesmerising football.

SILVER STARS:
If you weren't at the Arsenal game the only way you'd have seen the goals that day was on the news

A TASTE OF THINGS TO COME

Oxford turned Liverpool around to kick towards the Kop after winning the toss. That was their first error.

Tradition dictates that the Reds kick towards that end of the ground in the second half, but after waiting so long to see this Liverpool side, the noise inside Anfield was phenomenal. The 20,000 supporters on the Kop gave their players momentum.

Chants of 'Johnny Barnes, Johnny Barnes, Johnny Barnes' rang around before kick-off.

They wanted to see him running towards them in full flow. They wanted to see Beardsley jinking his way past his marker, Steve McMahon powering through midfield and the fit-again Steve Nicol bombing forward from full-back.

They wanted to see it so much that Liverpool's players couldn't fail to start at a high tempo. Oxford, with soon-to-be-signed Ray Houghton in midfield, were swamped.

Ronnie Whelan's volley was blocked. McMahon shot narrowly wide. A Barnes flick sent Alan Hansen running on to tee up Nicol, who blazed a shot just past the post.

With 13 minutes on the clock, Anfield was treated to the type of goal we'd all been dreaming of.

Beardsley, on the edge of his own penalty area, flicked the ball to Whelan, who sent Barnes racing away down the left. Seconds later, fox in the Ox's box Aldridge was turning Barnesy's inch-perfect cross in from close range – his first goal at the Kop end.

It was a sweeping move characterised by vision, pace and precision – three attributes we would see from this brilliant Liverpool team throughout the whole season – and the roar that greeted the goal was from a crowd wowed by what they were witnessing.

Beardsley – affectionately dubbed 'Quasi' on the Kop – and Barnes combined for Liverpool's second. The Reds' new number seven touched a free-kick into the path of our new number 10 and he brilliantly curled it around the Oxford wall and into the net.

The 'Johnny Barnes, Johnny Barnes' chants grew louder and louder. Anfield had a new hero, the best Reds winger since Stevie Heighway some suggested. He'd go on to earn legendary status.

There were no further goals after the break – the game finishing 2-0 – but we'd all seen enough to know Kenny's side could be something special. And they were.

For me, and no doubt for many of you reading, that class of '87/88 was the best Liverpool team to grace Anfield. It wasn't just that they won the league easily, it was how they won it. The pace, panache and flowing football they played was as good as anything seen from the Redmen. They were a joy to watch.

Twenty-five years on, we'll take you back through that unforgettable season, recalling the glorious goals, the stylish play and talking to the men who made it possible.

Only when you experience the bad times do you truly appreciate the good.

THE SEASON uncut >>

A month by month analysis of an outstanding season...

August 87

September 87

October 87

November 87

December 87

January 88

February 88

March 88

April 88

May 88

The season uncut

pre-season 1987/88

LIVERPOOL: THE 'CLASS' OF '87

AALBORG 75TH ANNIVERSARY FRIENDLY
July 26, Aalborg Stadium

Aalborg Chang 0
Liverpool 4
Aldridge 2 (1pen), Whelan, Barnes

Liverpool: Grobbelaar, Gillespie, Venison (Nicol), Ablett, Whelan (Magilton), Hansen, Walsh, Aldridge (Wark), Johnston, Beardsley, Barnes.

Attendance: 4,100

FRIENDLY
July 28, Ringsted Stadion

Broenshoej 1
scorer unknown
Liverpool 1
Nicol

Liverpool: Grobbelaar, Gillespie, Venison, Ablett, Nicol, Hansen, Dalglish (Aldridge), McMahon, Walsh, Spackman (Whelan), Barnes.

Attendance: 3,485

DIETER HOENESS TESTIMONIAL
July 23, Olympia Stadium

Bayern Munich 3
Matthaus, Hoeness, Wegmann
Liverpool 2
Aldridge, Barnes

Liverpool: Grobbelaar, Gillespie, Venison, Nicol, Whelan, Hansen, Beardsley, Johnston, Aldridge, Barnes, McMahon

Attendance: 25,000

FRIENDLY
August 3, Tingvalla IP

Karlstad BK 0
Liverpool 3
Beardsley, Aldridge (pen), Walsh

Liverpool: Grobbelaar, Gillespie, Spackman, Nicol, Whelan, Walsh (Dalglish), Beardsley, Johnston, Aldridge, Barnes, McMahon (Wark).

Attendance: 5,567

FRIENDLY
August 6, Bislett Stadium

Valerenga 1
scorer unknown
Liverpool 4
Aldridge 3 (1pen), Walsh

Liverpool: Grobbelaar, Venison, Nicol, Johnston, Whelan, Hansen, Beardsley (Dalglish), Walsh, Aldridge, Wark, Barnes (McMahon)

Attendance: 7,275

FRIENDLY
August 1, Spjald Stadion

Vejle 0
Liverpool 3
Aldridge, Beardsley, Johnston

Liverpool: Grobbelaar, Gillespie (Spackman), Venison, Nicol, Whelan, Hansen, Beardsley, Aldridge, Johnston, Barnes, McMahon (Wark).

Attendance: 2,600

TOMMY BURNS TESTIMONIAL
August 9, Parkhead

Celtic 0
Liverpool 1
Whelan

Liverpool: Grobbelaar, Gillespie, Venison, Nicol, Whelan, Hansen, Walsh (Dalglish), Aldridge (Beardsley), Johnston, Barnes, McMahon.

Attendance: 42,000

august 1987

STARTING UNDER PRESSURE

The season began with the league championship trophy resting on the other side of Stanley Park and new signings desperate to make a big impact. The Reds needed to throw down the gauntlet early...

LIVERPOOL went into the opening month of the season in good condition even if there were concerns around Anfield about the year ahead.

The summer had seen the goalscoring legend Ian Rush leave for Juventus and Peter Beardsley and John Barnes arrive.

Kenny Dalglish had, at least for those times, spent a fortune by splashing £900,000 on Barnes from Watford and a record £1.9m on Beardsley from Newcastle United.

On top of those fresh buys, John Aldridge had arrived from Oxford United halfway through the season before in a bid to replace Rush – whose deal to move to Turin had been rubber-stamped by the time his look-alike made the move to his boyhood club.

The money spent then seems nothing compared with what is spent now but the Liverpool manager was under pressure to justify his use of the chequebook – especially as he also announced that he would only occasionally play himself from now on.

For a club that prided itself so heavily on its financial security and how efficiently it did business, the fact the Reds were spending so heavily raised a few eyebrows.

Only a good start to the season ahead would calm down those who believed Liverpool had panicked following Rush's departure.

On top of that, the other side of Stanley Park was rejoicing after Everton's successful league campaign the year before.

The Blues were the champions of England and that brought its own pressure.

Liverpool simply could not allow their near neighbours to steal their spot as Merseyside – and England's – most dominant club.

August was not only an important month for the Reds in the league, they also did the business in that long-forgotten footballing tradition: the friendly during the season.

Liverpool played two friendlies in August, a 5-0 victory over an Irish Olympic XI at Lansdowne Road followed by a 1-0 win over Atletico Madrid at the Vicente Calderon.

Both games passed without incident. Well almost. Liverpool's team bus had a minor prang ahead of the Madrid match and, fortunately for Dalglish, that was his biggest worry all month – even if he did have a lot to ponder.

In the league he needed his men to provide both the perfect start and the perfect way to silence the detractors.

So as local boy Rick Astley blared out "Never Gonna Give You Up" Kenny Dalglish was hoping his men were never gonna let him down.

They didn't.

Barclays Football League
Division One
Saturday, August 15
Highbury

Arsenal 1
Davis 17

Liverpool 2
Aldridge 9, Nicol 88

Arsenal: Lukic, Thomas, Sansom, Williams, O'Leary, Adams, Rocastle (Groves 75), Davis, Smith, Nicholas, Hayes.

Liverpool: Grobbelaar, Gillespie, Venison, Nicol, Whelan, Hansen, Beardsley (Walsh 85), Aldridge, Johnston, Barnes, McMahon.

Attendance: 54,703

Uncut fact:
Liverpool wore their new all-silver away strip for the first time.

A MAGNIFICENT header by Steve Nicol only two minutes from time gave Liverpool a dramatic victory at Highbury, after they had led through John Aldridge and then seen Paul Davis snatch an equaliser.

Liverpool's new-look attack in their new-look silver strip did not take long to hit the target.

Only nine minutes had passed when Aldridge headed in a cross from John Barnes, after Peter Beardsley had been involved in the build-up.

Arsenal counter-attacked with tremendous determination and Liverpool had to withstand almost a non-stop siege.

They seemed to be weathering the storm but in the 17th minute Arsenal drew level when Charlie Nicholas crossed from the left, Alan Smith headed the ball forward and Davis was there to head it into the net.

The game could have gone either way in the second half on a sweltering afternoon in the capital, but with two minutes to go Nicol put Liverpool in front again with a magnificent header from the edge of the box after Tony Adams cleared a free-kick by Barnes.

It got Kenny Dalglish's men off to a fine start to the season and proved that when it comes to scoring goals there will be life without Ian Rush - something the rest of the First Division must have feared.

v Arsenal

THE OTHER GAME WASN'T BAD EITHER...

Barclays Football League
Division One
Saturday, August 29
Highfield Road

Coventry City 1
Regis 88

Liverpool 4
Nicol 20, 49, Aldridge 52pen, Beardsley 83

A BRACE from Steve Nicol plus further strikes from John Aldridge and Peter Beardsley ensured Liverpool made it two wins from two.

Coventry had no answer as the Reds ran riot at Highfield Road although a late Cyrille Regis goal for the home side did spare some blushes.

Coventry: Ogrizovic, Borrows, Downs (Phillips), McGrath, Kilcline, Peake, Bennett, Gynn (Houchen), Regis, Speedie, Pickering.
Liverpool: Grobbelaar, Gillespie, Venison, Nicol, Whelan, Hansen, Beardsley, Aldridge (Walsh 81), Johnston, Barnes, McMahon.

Attendance: 27,637

Uncut fact:
Peter Beardsley scored his first goal for Liverpool.

FIRST OF MANY: Peter Beardsley grabbed his first goal for the Reds in the 4-1 win at Coventry City

august 1987

NIC-KING IT: Steve Nicol's headed winner is from so far out he's not even in shot as the ball loops over Arsenal keeper John Lukic

11

BRIAN READE

THE NATIONAL NEWSPAPER COLUMNIST AND LIFELONG
KOPITE REFLECTS ON A SIDE THAT TOOK EXPECTATIONS
OF WHAT A GREAT TEAM SHOULD BE TO A NEW LEVEL

OOZING QUALITY:
The 1987/88 squad were
admired as well as feared

'I'D SEEN GAMES IN WHICH
LIVERPOOL HAD DEMOLISHED
RIVALS (THE 1974 FA CUP
FINAL AND THE 7-0 ROUT OF
SPURS) BUT THIS TEAM PUT
THOSE SHOWS ON ALMOST
AS A MATTER-OF-FACT.
THEIR SUPREMACY WAS AS
GLORIOUS FOR US AS IT WAS
EMBARRASSING FOR EVERY
OTHER TEAM'

BY the time I'd turned 29, in 1986, I believed I'd seen it all. As I told every non-Kopite who challenged my smugness, I wasn't being big-headed, just truthful.

Since first going to Anfield in 1965 I'd watched Liverpool win 10 league titles, four European Cups, three FA Cups, four League Cups and two UEFA Cups. I'd drooled over the skills of St John and Hunt, Keegan and Heighway, Dalglish and Souness, soaked in the wit and wisdom of Shankly and Paisley, entered Wembley without paying more times than the Coldstream Guards and sang and danced from Paris to Rome with the most entertaining band of troubadours on earth.

By the time I turned 30, in 1987, I realised I was wrong.

From the August of that year I'd been watching something I'd never seen before. Something quite extraordinary, quite sublime. Poetry in red motion. The most beautiful football a Liverpool team had ever played. Beauty I'm still waiting to see surpassed.

The least forgettable rides are enriched by the drabness of

the previous journey, and 1986/87 was as dour as it got for Liverpool fans of that era.

After winning the 1986 double we felt we'd make up for the post-Heysel European ban by scooping everything in sight domestically. But Everton won the league title and we lost the League Cup final to Arsenal, after Ian Rush had scored (which was literally unheard of).

At the end of the season Kenny Dalglish effectively hung up his boots and, even worse, Rushie was off to Juventus. With nobody at that point realising he'd get so homesick for Heinz Beans he'd be back in a year.

We needed a cavalry to rescue us from what threatened to be another trophy-less season. And in the shape of John Aldridge (who arrived early), Peter Beardsley, John Barnes and Ray Houghton (who arrived late) it came over the hill.

No-one would have guessed it at the time, but it turned out to be the greatest construction of a Liverpool quartet since Brian Epstein put the Beatles together.

The city had found another four boys to shake the world. At a combined cost of £4.3 million. Or one-eighth of an Andy Carroll (plus change).

They gelled immediately with the core of the side – Alan Hansen, Gary Gillespie, Steve Nicol, Ronnie Whelan and Steve McMahon – to produce, on a weekly basis, football of breath-taking fluidity.

It was the closest we'd ever known to the perfection watched by Real Madrid fans in the early 60s, and Ajax in the early 70s. More importantly, it was our answer to those who claimed the best Manchester United sides had always played sumptuous football while Liverpool's were simply relentless trophy-winning machines built to Germanic standards.

Whether we admitted it or not, the truth was, up to that point our great teams had been more admired and feared by neutrals, than loved.

We never reached the aesthetic heights of Best, Charlton and Law (as anyone who saw them thrash us 4-1 at Anfield in 1969 can testify). Our clinical efficiency, the Shankly/ Paisley intolerance of "fancy-Dans" and the mantra of collective effort above individualism, had never taken the nation's breath away.

The class of '87/88 did. Week after week after week.

I'd seen games in which Liverpool had demolished rivals (the 1974 FA Cup Final against Newcastle and the 7-0 rout of Spurs in 1978 stand out) but this team put those shows on almost as a matter-of-fact. Their supremacy was as glorious for us as it was embarrassing for the rest of the country.

Much of the praise has to go to Kenny

EYE WITNESS: Brian Reade looked on as established stars like Alan Hansen blended perfectly with new blood like John Aldridge (above) who arrived early in 1987

13

Dalglish. History re-writers who weren't enamoured with his second time in charge, who say he inherited a smooth-running Mercedes first time around and simply added the oil, are wrong.

Compare the first league team he picked as manager in 1985 (Grobbelaar, Neal, Kennedy; Lawrenson, Whelan, Hansen; Dalglish, Nicol, Rush, Molby, Beglin) with the one that started the 1987 season (Grobbelaar, Gillespie, Venison; Nicol, Whelan, Hansen; Beardsley, Aldridge, Johnston, Barnes, McMahon) and you'll see only four players had survived (Grobbelaar, Nicol, Whelan and Hansen). Plus Ray Houghton would soon force out Craig Johnston.

This 1987/88 team was unquestionably Dalglish's. In personnel and in character. It had his charisma and intelligence stamped all over it.

Dalglish liberated Liverpool, and in doing so took the club to new heights. We remained solid and effective in the

'I FIRST REALISED SOMETHING SPECIAL WAS UNFOLDING DURING THE SECOND GAME OF THE SEASON, AT COVENTRY, WHEN WE TORE THEM APART, 4-1, WITHOUT GETTING OUT OF THIRD GEAR'

middle, but round the edges we let rip. With Barnes and Beardsley we had players who were encouraged to express themselves at every opportunity.

And I had the perfect view of it all, having moved to the Kemlyn Road from the Kop, after a mate stopped growing upwards and spread sideways. Ten rows from the front, to the left of the half-way line, I had a close-up view of one of the all-time great Anfield sights: A goal-bound John Barnes in full flow.

It was majesty personified. I'd been lucky enough to see both Peter Thompson and Steve Heighway, and at the peak of their powers their dribbling ability at pace was mesmeric. But Barnes, even at 24, had an extra dimension to his game.

With the build of a boxer and the feet of a ballet dancer, he had an athletic guile that set him apart. Daley Thompson in footie boots.

He was like a matador, drawing a defender in, pushing the ball through him, bursting past, doing it to the next defender, before whipping a cross in for Aldridge or planting it in the top corner himself.

We'd never seen a Brazilian in a red kit before, but here was our Pele. Our very own black pearl.

His finest goal, and the one that sums up the season in these eyes, came against QPR in October.

He picked the ball up on the half-way line, coaxed a hapless defender on to

his wrong foot, then waltzed past him, threw the shoulder, shimmied past another, turned one inside out, then another, as he weaved towards the Kop, and suddenly without looking, steered it across the bemused keeper into his top left-hand corner.

It was one of those instances where your brain struggles to keep up with what your eyes are seeing. A piece of genius.

Forget his legendary goal against Brazil at the Maracana. This, to me, was Barnes' best strike. The kind of goal that only served to remind Liverpudlians that the more England fans gave him stick, the more we loved him.

I first realised something special was unfolding during

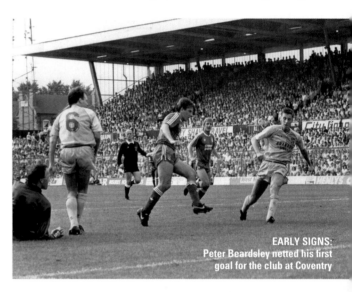

EARLY SIGNS:
Peter Beardsley netted his first goal for the club at Coventry

the second game of the season, at Coventry, when we tore them apart, 4-1, without getting out of third gear.

The red army that descended that day headed back home drooling at the prospect of what was in store. The league became a formality way before the unbeaten 29-game run ended at Everton.

If ever a title was won at a canter, this was it. A club record 90 points was reached, nine ahead of Man United, whose 21-year title drought would stretch to another five years. There didn't seem to be a single cloud on the horizon.

The odd regret though. Mainly that we were banned from Europe. The prospect of this team terrifying the continent's best the way it had done across England, was mouth-watering.

Who knows what it could have led to? But it wasn't to be, and those of us who were at Heysel understood more than most exactly why.

The game that went down in legend as the one that typified that season was the 5-0 thumping of Nottingham Forest. Better qualified men than me (Shankly's favourite player of all-time Tom Finney, for one) called this the complete footballing performance.

All I can remember is spending most of the 90 minutes with my jaw open, and leaving Anfield, like the rest of my mates, stuck for words. Plus, I was probably one of the few Liverpool fans that night cursing.

Since early September I'd put money on them to win most

games 4-0, and cleaned up six times. A fifth goal against Forest meant my bet was down that night.

A few weeks later another one would go down in embarrassing fashion. Along with the Double.

On FA Cup Final morning I walked past a bookies in central London, and took offence that the window display was showing no odds on us beating Wimbledon by more than 4-0.

I went in, and asked for his price on 6-0. He came back with 100/1 and a smirk. Then took my money. And probably didn't stop smirking for a week.

I'd like to say that losing 1-0 to Wimbledon didn't really matter, because it didn't really hurt. But it did. Because it did.

But that freak result against the Crazy Gang can't stop me, and I'm guessing every Liverpudlian who was lucky enough to have been a part of that glorious season, from looking back at 1987/88 with anything but a big smile.

Accompanied by the words from that well-known Dingle crooner Terry (brother of Barry and Garry) Jacks:

"We had joy we had fun, we'd a season in the sun,
And the peaks that we climbed gave us all the greatest time."

SHOCK: One of the biggest surprises in football saw the Reds beaten by Wimbledon in the FA Cup Final – just weeks after Liverpool's 5-0 demolition of Nottingham Forest

TRIUMPH: The players celebrate our 17th title at Anfield

september 1987

THE GOALS START FLOWING

John Aldridge's exhibition of master marksmanship helps Kopites cope with the loss of Rushie, but Steve Nicol is the surprise package as seven goals in seven games help get Reds off to a flyer

LIVERPOOL'S players and fans could easily have been suffering a serious bout of home sickness in September as refurbishments to the Kop ensured the season was almost a month old before the Reds played at Anfield.

But it was already clear that Liverpool were going to be made of sterner stuff this year.

Before that first appearance at home, Liverpool's mettle was tested at West Ham while Mark Lawrenson also showed signs that his nightmare achilles injury was finally coming to an end as he played several reserve games and inched his way back into contention.

One bonus in Liverpool's eventual Anfield opener against Oxford United was the opportunity it gave Kenny Dalglish and his back-room staff to take a close look at a certain midfielder who went by the name of Ray Houghton.

The Reds may have dominated proceedings but Houghton's own performance was not to be forgotten by Dalglish – and Liverpool's fans grew to be ever more thankful for that as the season progressed...

As the month went on, Lawrenson was finally fit enough to come back in to the side for Liverpool's narrow win over Charlton Athletic and his return was welcomed by all.

Players of Lawrenson's skill and experience are not to be found around every corner.

Talking of skilful players, John Aldridge's September underlined how undaunted he was about the task of trying to replace Ian Rush.

When one lithe, moustached killer-instinct-type striker is replaced by another the chances of them not being compared are minimal.

The Reds tried to deny Aldridge was a like-for-like replacement for Rush but he didn't help matters in September. Why? Because he did nothing but score goals like Rushie used to.

In fact, Aldridge's goal against Newcastle meant he had netted in seven successive Liverpool games – one more than even the great Welshman managed.

However, Aldridge's scoring exploits were being outshone by the most unlikely of players - Steve Nicol.

A hat-trick against Newcastle and another goal against Blackburn helped him to the astonishing stat of seven goals in as many games so far. Not bad for a defender eh. And maybe all the evidence Reds fans needed that this year would indeed be something out of the ordinary.

In the year car company Ford took a shareholding in Aston Martin, the Reds' engine was purring beautifully as the season began.

Barclays Football League
Division One
Sunday, September 20
St James' Park

Newcastle United 1
McDonald 61

Liverpool 4
Nicol 20, 47, 70, Aldridge 37

WHEN it comes to skill and entertainment the South Americans know a thing or two. So the brief summing up by Mirandinha at the end of this game should have been taken as the highest compliment by everyone at Anfield.

The tiny Tyneside hero had just witnessed a Liverpool performance at St. James' Park which was as fluent as any Brazilian blend, incorporating a magnificent Steve Nicol hat-trick, and said: "They are a great team. They know how to use space so well and they don't miss much." Short and sweet.

This was Peter Beardsley's first return to Newcastle since he packed his bags in the summer and the match had been billed as a battle between him and Mirandinha. But we should have known better. Liverpool are a team, not just a collection of great players.

Beardsley, booed as his name was announced on the tannoy but cheered at the end of play, fared well without hitting top form. There were plenty of other occasions that season when he did.

Once again it was on the flanks where the Reds were outstanding.

Down the right, Nicol provided watching Scotland boss Andy Roxburgh with more options for his team with his first senior treble, the opening goal coming after 20 minutes when Anderson cut out Barnes' cross, but inadvertently played the ball into Nicol's path and the Scot swept it home.

Barnes, Liverpool's "Brazilian", had linked superbly with Beardsley on the left, and throughout the game he showed skill worthy of a Garrincha or Amarildo. His display earned praise from Mirandinha: "He's a very good player. He's like a South American when he gets the ball and that was one of the features of the game."

By half-time the Reds were two-up, courtesy of a well-poached goal by Aldridge after Barnes had headed back Venison's deep cross.

If Willie McFaul had given his side a pep-talk at half-time then it was wasted within two minutes of the restart as Beardsley's inch-perfect pass was finished off by Nicol.

Neil McDonald pulled one back for Newcastle from the penalty spot after referee Keith Hackett decided that Gary Gillespie had fouled Mirandinha but Liverpool's three-goal advantage was restored by Nicol when he brilliantly chipped the keeper to make it 4-1 to the Reds.

Newcastle: Kelly, McDonald, Anderson, McCreery, P Jackson, Roeder, Stephenson, Wharton, Mirandinha, Goddard, Hodges (D Jackson).
Liverpool: Grobbelaar, Gillespie (Spackman 74), Venison, Nicol, Whelan, Hansen, Beardsley, Aldridge, Lawrenson, Barnes, McMahon.

Attendance: 24,141

Uncut fact:
This was Liverpool's first live televised game of the season and Steve Nicol's only hat-trick for the club.

SNIFFING OUT A GOAL: John Aldridge didn't hit the net with this header, but he did score with his feet in the 4-1 win on Tyneside

STORY OF THE MONTH

Barclays Football League
Division One
Saturday, September 5
Upton Park

West Ham 1
Cottee 75

Liverpool 1
Aldridge 50pen

A BLUNDER from Alan Hansen ended Liverpool's 100 per cent record as West Ham United escaped with a draw against the Reds.

Liverpool were the better side at Upton Park and should have won easily, but missed several chances.

John Aldridge scored an early second half penalty and that seemed to be enough for Kenny's men, but a wayward backpass from Hansen was pounced upon by Tony Cottee and he rounded Bruce Grobbelaar to earn the Hammers an unlikely draw.

West Ham: McAllister, Stewart, McQueen (Parris 20), Strodder, Martin, Brady, Ward, McAvennie, Ince, Cottee, Robson.
Liverpool: Grobbelaar, Gillespie, Venison, Nicol, Whelan, Hansen, Beardsley, Aldridge, Spackman, Barnes, McMahon.

Attendance: 29,865

Uncut fact:
Kenny Dalglish made his first selection change of the season, bringing in Nigel Spackman for the injured Craig Johnston.

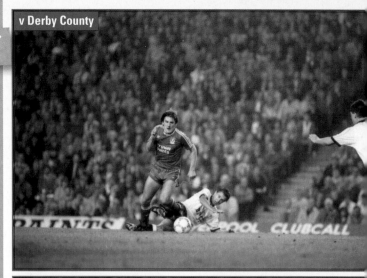

v Derby County

Barclays Football League
Division One
Saturday, September 12
Anfield

Liverpool 2
Aldridge 13, Barnes 37

Oxford United 0

LIVERPOOL celebrated their return to Anfield after a Kop sewer collapse with a comfortable victory over Oxford inspired by John Barnes on his home debut.

John Aldridge scored Liverpool's first after 13 minutes as he finished off Barnes' clever cross before the winger added a second with a brilliant curling left foot shot from a free-kick.

Liverpool: Grobbelaar, Gillespie, Venison, Nicol, Whelan, Hansen, Beardsley, Aldridge (Walsh 73), Spackman, Barnes, McMahon (Wark 83).
Oxford: Hucker, Slatter, Dreyer, Shelton, Briggs, Caton, Houghton, Foyle, Whitehurst, Hebberd, Saunders (Phillips).

Attendance: 42,266

Uncut fact:
John Barnes became the third player to net on his Anfield debut in 1987, following John Aldridge (February) and Gary Ablett (April).

Barclays Football League
Division One
Tuesday, September 15
Anfield

Liverpool 3
Aldridge 9pen, Hansen 71, McMahon 73

Charlton 2
Crooks 8, Walsh 59

THE Reds launched a late fightback to break brave Charlton's hearts in a thrilling 3-2 encounter.

Goals from Garth Crooks and Colin Walsh, either side of a John Aldridge penalty, twice gave the Addicks shock leads.

However, Liverpool underlined their championship credentials thanks to an Alan Hansen diving header and Steve McMahon's Kop end winner.

Liverpool: Grobbelaar, Gillespie, Venison, Nicol, Whelan, Hansen, Beardsley, Aldridge, Spackman (Lawrenson 60), Barnes, McMahon.
Charlton: Johns, Humphrey, Gritt, Peake, Shirtliff, Miller, Milne (Williams), Stuart, Walsh, Mackenzie, Crooks.

Attendance: 36,637

Uncut fact:
Alan Hansen's Kop end header was his first goal since May 1984 and his last for Liverpool FC.

18

TREBLE-TASTIC: John Aldridge hit his first Liverpool hat-trick in the 4-0 home win against Derby

v West Ham United

AT ARMS' LENGTH: Aldo found the net at West Ham but the home side snatched a 1-1 draw

v Oxford United

HOMECOMING: The Reds' number eight showed no mercy to his former club in the long-awaited first Anfield game of the season

---

Littlewoods Cup
second round, first leg
Wednesday, September 23
Ewood Park

Blackburn Rovers 1
Sellars 49

Liverpool 1
Nicol 30

STEVE Nicol's fine goalscoring start to the season continued but Liverpool could not overcome a determined Blackburn Rovers at Ewood Park.

The Second Division club gave a good account of themselves, although it was the Reds who squandered most of the chances.

Nicol gave Liverpool the lead after half an hour but Scott Sellars equalised early in the second half and Bruce Grobbelaar prevented a Simon Garner winner.

Blackburn: Gennoe, Price, Sulley, Barker (Millar), Hill, Mail, Gayle (Miller), Reid, Curry, Garner, Sellars.
Liverpool: Grobbelaar, Spackman, Venison, Nicol, Whelan, Hansen, Beardsley (Walsh 70), Aldridge, Lawrenson, Barnes, McMahon.

Attendance: 13,924

Uncut fact:
Before the game, Reserve defender Mark Seagraves was sold to Man City for £100,000 after just two appearances for Liverpool.

Barclays Football League
Division One
Tuesday, September 29
Anfield

Liverpool 4
Aldridge 41pen, 68pen, 73, Beardsley 47

Derby County 0

JOHN Aldridge's hat-trick helped the Reds blow Derby away at Anfield.

Liverpool took a 1-0 lead into the break courtesy of an Aldridge penalty but Dalglish's men turned the screw in the second half.

Aldo claimed the match ball with two further goals past Peter Shilton while Peter Beardsley also chipped in his first home goal as Liverpool ran riot.

Liverpool: Grobbelaar, Gillespie, Venison, Nicol (Lawrenson 78), Whelan, Hansen, Beardsley, Aldridge, Johnston (Walsh 85), Barnes, McMahon.
Derby: Shilton, Blades, Forsyth, Williams, Wright, MacLaren, Sage, Gee (Garner), Davison, Gregory, Callaghan.

Attendance: 43,405

Uncut fact:
John Aldridge netted his first hat-trick of three hat-tricks for the club to put Liverpool second, three points behind leaders QPR who had played two games more.

THREE OF THE BEST SHIRTS

The popularity of a Reds shirt is linked with how fondly remembered the team that played in it were. Many great memories come flooding back whenever fans see these classic adidas-crown paints combos

KIT DESIGN	KIT SPONSORS
adidas®	crown paints

ABOUT THE KIT

New home, away and third kits were launched in '87/88. The classic all-red home shirt saw the return of the round neck white collar while the three white stripes were extended right down the sleeves, giving it a classic adidas look. Up close you could also see vertical panels bearing the Liver bird and adidas logo. The hint of yellow on the previous home strip was now removed completely - to be replaced by a silver/grey trim. The badge also changed, with the traditional Liver bird on both shirt and shorts now sitting inside a crest - which wasn't a popular choice with everyone. The shorts included the familiar three white stripes down the sides, with the white stripes also on the sock turn-ups - with an adidas logo centred in the socks.

This was also the season when the silver/grey away kit was introduced, an ambitious but successful leap from the traditional whites and yellows of the past. It retained the same design as the home version. In the event, two away strips had to be produced after the initial white sponsor with red trim was replaced with solid red letters so it could be seen better.

WHITE SPONSOR

A rare sighting on the grey/silver away strip, the 'crown paints' sponsor was changed to red to make it more prominent.

CUP FINAL SHIRT

Like previous finals when adidas sponsored the kit, it would be around the sportswear manufacturer's logo where the commemorative cup final message was written on the shirt.

THIRD CHOICE

Despite no obvious clash with the silver/grey away strip, this kit was worn by the Reds at Aston Villa in the FA Cup fourth round tie of January 1988. Utilising the home shorts and socks, the shirt was the white worn as an away colour in the previous two seasons - including the 1987 League Cup final. Relegated to third choice, it still did the trick as Liverpool won a tricky encounter 2-0.

DID YOU KNOW?

John Aldridge was the first and last player to score in Liverpool's new silver-grey away strip. He found the net in the ninth minute at Highbury on the opening day of the season as Kenny Dalglish's men beat Arsenal 2-1 and netted a 70th-minute penalty during a 2-1 defeat at Nottingham Forest's City Ground in April. It was the only game Liverpool lost while wearing their away strip during the 1987/88 campaign.

october 1987

FOURS
TO RECKON WITH

The goals keep coming as the Reds hit top spot for the first time – and with another high class midfielder recruited, the progress of Kenny's men was already looking ominous for the rest of the league

WHILE this may have been the month of Black Monday, Liverpool kept dishing out Black Saturdays to their opponents.

By October it was becoming brutally clear that nothing was going to stop the Reds when they were in the mood to cause chaos.

The month's opening game against Portsmouth saw the Anfield visitors adopt a super-negative approach. Five defenders, barely any strikers, even less ambition.

They arrived with a point and manager Alan Ball was convinced they would leave with a point.

The former Everton star was wrong. Badly wrong.

Liverpool began the month against Pompey by again netting four times – the fourth time in just nine league games they had managed it.

Dalglish's men were erupting at will, scoring for fun, playing with a smile on their faces that was only matched by the cheers from the crowd.

A League Cup win over Blackburn saw Liverpool pitted against Everton in the third round – a draw that saw every other side with silverware ambitions rejoice at the thought that one of the country's two best sides would not be going any further.

Before that tie, a called-off match at waterlogged Wimbledon frustrated the Reds' momentum although another 4-0 win, this time in a testimonial against Dundee, ensured Liverpool's sharpshooters remained focused.

Halfway through

the month, Dalglish's previous admiration of Ray Houghton's skills was confirmed as the midfielder was recruited for £800,000 from Oxford United.

The Manor Ground had provided rich pickings for Dalglish as Houghton joined former Oxford frontman Aldridge on Merseyside. And Houghton was to impress and prosper in the same way.

Another 4-0 victory over QPR – who were league leaders at the time – plus a 1-0 win over Luton Town were enjoyable but they were then followed by a 1-0 defeat to Everton in the Littlewoods Cup.

That was a slight blip but when it came to league performances, Liverpool bounced through October still unbeaten, still looking mean, still looking like champions-elect.

No titles are won after less than three months and 20 games but, just as jockey Lester Piggott **(pictured)** was being jailed for tax fraud, the Reds were looking odds-on favourites for the title several furlongs from home. No Liverpool team in recent memory had looked so ominous, so dangerous, so ambitious.

GAME OF THE MONTH

Barclays Football League
Division One
Saturday, October 17
Anfield

Liverpool 4
Johnston 41, Aldridge 65pen, Barnes 79, 85

QPR 0

JIM SMITH, old bald eagle himself, was still chirping away at Anfield despite being knocked off his prospective title perch by the real championship favourites.

The Queens Park Rangers boss was trying to be positive after the 4-0 defeat that cost his side the top spot for the first time all season.

There were those who claimed Rangers' championship dreams were as plastic as their pitch. Smith was right to nail those accusations as QPR kept Liverpool in their sights for about an hour until a disputed penalty, crashed home by John Aldridge, finally turned this game into a romp.

It was a signal for John Barnes to take centre stage, enhancing his growing reputation as the most skilful, enthralling attacker in the business with another double of the highest class.

In a tense first half, Liverpool always had the advantage and when they finally broke the deadlock three minutes before the interval it was fitting that the goalscorer was the lively Craig Johnston who pounced from close range after Barnes cut back a hard and low cross from the left.

Rangers pushed their full-backs Ian Dawes and Warren Neill forward whenever possible and when they linked in the 50th minute Bruce Grobbelaar was alert to Dawes' volley.

Liverpool had to be patient in an effort to draw their opponents but after 65 minutes Dean Coney handled a Barnes centre in a packed goalmouth and Aldridge slotted home the penalty with ease.

They set up a memorable finale as Barnes made it 3-0 12 minutes from time after a one-two with Aldridge. The winger then capped an astonishing display with a cool finish after a mesmerising run had the QPR defence trailing in his wake.

The Bald Eagle had to bow to the Liver bird. Rangers' reign at the top was over.

Liverpool: Grobbelaar, Gillespie, Venison, Nicol, Whelan, Hansen, Beardsley, Aldridge, Johnston (Walsh 86), Barnes, McMahon (Lawrenson 86).
QPR: Seaman, Neill (Pizanti 77), Dawes, Parker, McDonald, Fenwick, Allen, Coney (Maguire 77), Bannister, Byrne, Brock.

Attendance: 43,735

Uncut fact:
John Aldridge scored in his 10th consecutive league match, a club record that still stands today.

ON TOP: Craig Johnston opens the scoring against QPR as the Reds asserted their authority

Barclays Football League
Division One
Saturday, October 3
Anfield

Liverpool 4
*Beardsley 30, McMahon 50,
Aldridge 52pen, Whelan 71*
Portsmouth 0

LIVERPOOL made it back-to-back 4-0 wins at home with Portsmouth trounced in their first Division One visit to Anfield for 34 years.

Just four days after battering the Rams by the same scoreline, Pompey were on the receiving end.

Peter Beardsley opened the scoring, Steve McMahon made it two and further strikes from John Aldridge and Ronnie Whelan underlined the Reds' awesome potential.

Liverpool: Grobbelaar, Gillespie, Venison, Nicol, Whelan, Hansen, Beardsley, Aldridge, Johnston (Lawrenson 66), Barnes, McMahon (Walsh 76).
Portsmouth: Knight, Swain, Sandford, Fillery (Dillon), Shotton, Gilbert (Ball), Horne, Whitehead, Mariner, Quinn, Hilaire.

Attendance: 44,366

Uncut fact:
Pompey boss Alan Ball tried to stop John Barnes by detailing Barry Horne to mark him man-to-man. It didn't work.

Littlewoods Cup
second round, second leg
Tuesday, October 6
Anfield

Liverpool 1
Aldridge 89
Blackburn Rovers 0

JOHN ALDRIDGE left it late as Blackburn's brave League Cup resistance finally ended at Anfield.

After holding the Reds to a 1-1 draw in the first leg, Liverpool's class finally shone through as John Aldridge headed a winner just 90 seconds from the end of this tight encounter.

Liverpool: Grobbelaar, Gillespie, Venison, Nicol, Whelan, Hansen, Beardsley, Aldridge, Johnston, Barnes, Wark (Lawrenson 64).
Blackburn: Gennoe, Price, Sulley, Barker, Hendry, Dawson, Mail, Reid, Curry, Garner, Sellars.

Attendance: 28,994

Uncut fact:
John Wark started his first game of the season in what turned out to be his last appearance for Liverpool.

GARY GILLESP-GLEE: The big defender angles a pass on a big day for the Reds as they took over from QPR at the top of the table – but it was John Barnes' contribution that lives longest in the memory

v QPR

v Everton (Littlewoods Cup)

New boy joins in

WELCOME DINNER: Ray Houghton with some of his new team-mates after joining from Oxford United

Barclays Football League
Division One
Saturday, October 24
Kenilworth Road

Luton Town 0

Liverpool 1
Gillespie 71

GARY Gillespie secured the three points for Liverpool with a second-half finish at Kenilworth Road.

It was an important win for Dalglish's side on Luton's infamous plastic pitch which the Reds boss had often criticised.

Big Gillespie's header earned the victory, but Kenny's concerns were underlined by an Achilles injury to Barry Venison that kept him out of action for the following two months.

Luton: Sealey, Breacker, Grimes, McDonough, Foster, Donaghy, Wilson, Stein, Harford, Allinson, Weir.
Liverpool: Grobbelaar, Gillespie, Venison, Nicol, Whelan, Hansen, Beardsley, Aldridge, Houghton, Barnes, McMahon (Lawrenson 86).

Attendance: 12,452

Uncut fact:
Ray Houghton made his Liverpool debut after an £800,000 transfer from Oxford which was only agreed to by U's owner Robert Maxwell if his newspaper, the Daily Mirror, could exclusively break the story!

october 1987

DRAWING A BLANK: The Reds suffered their first defeat of the season in the Littlewoods Cup loss to Everton

Littlewoods Cup
third round
Wednesday, October 28
Anfield

Liverpool 0

Everton 1
Stevens 83

LIVERPOOL'S first loss of the season came at the hands of arch-rivals Everton.

A deflected Gary Stevens finish with seven minutes left proved to be enough to knock the Reds out of the Littlewoods Cup.

Liverpool: Grobbelaar, Gillespie, Lawrenson, Nicol, Whelan, Hansen, Beardsley, Aldridge, Johnston, Barnes, McMahon.
Everton: Southall, Stevens, van den Hauwe, Ratcliffe, Watson, Reid, Steven, Heath, Sharp, Snodin, Wilson.

Attendance: 44,071

Uncut fact:
Anfield was a sell-out for this League Cup tie while an estimated crowd of 30,000 also watched the game on a giant screen at Goodison Park.

KENNY DALGLISH

THE MANAGER OF THAT GREAT '87/88 TEAM REFLECTS ON THE COMPONENTS THAT CAME TOGETHER TO PRODUCE A DRESSING ROOM FULL OF GREAT CHARACTERS AND EQUALLY GREAT PLAYERS

'IT WAS UNUSUAL FOR LIVERPOOL TO HAVE NEW PLAYERS COMING STRAIGHT INTO THE FIRST-TEAM. FOR THOSE LADS TO SETTLE SO QUICKLY WAS A GREAT CREDIT TO THEM'

Kenny Dalglish is the last person you should ask if the team he steered to a magnificent 1987-88 championship success deserved the tag: 'Better than the Brazilians!'

He fills with pride at the very thought, but his first instinct is to consider the wider picture and the Liverpool the world of football grew to admire and seek to emulate between 1959 and 1987, inspired by icons like the great Bill Shankly, the modest – but supremely successful – Bob Paisley and the hugely respected Joe Fagan.

Kenny puts it this way: "I have never been involved with any Liverpool team as a player or a manager that did not have a hunger and a desire to win trophies."

In other words, he is not about to debate any suggestion that his late Eighties team was better than anything that had gone before. That is for other people to judge.

What Kenny knows and extols at every opportunity is the fact that in 1977 he came down from Glasgow to join a club that was a world football force at that time, but which carried that tag with a modesty and respect for others that many lesser clubs in our modern world of greed, celebrity and self interest would do well to study, grasp and understand.

By the time he had become Liverpool's first player-

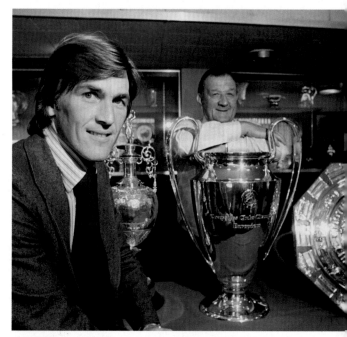

TRADITION OF HUMILITY: Kenny, pictured after signing for the Reds in 1977, learned a lot from previous managers like Bob Paisley

manager in the summer of 1985, Kenny had already won three European Cups at Anfield, five championships, the European Super Cup, and four League Cups. That's a remarkable amount of silverware by any standards.

But in his first seven years with the club, you suspect the things Kenny treasured more than anything were the lessons and the values laid down by his predecessors. He didn't play for Shanks, but he knew everything about him, no doubt being told many times about his fellow Scot by the equally legendary Jock Stein of Celtic.

Of course, Kenny was signed by Bob Paisley and what a piece of business that turned out to be. Kenny would ultimately feel huge pride, tinged with sadness, at being the man chosen to replace Joe Fagan, who struggled to come to terms with the aftermath of Heysel.

Having accepted the job, Kenny knew that if something wasn't broken, there was no need to tamper with it, and so his early transfer activity was fairly modest in 1985.

One great signing was that of Steve McMahon from Aston Villa for £350,000. The former Everton man was mobile and a great tackler. He could also score crucial goals. A less modest but important bit of business was to add goalkeeping cover with the acquisition of Mike Hooper from Wrexham for £40,000. Liverpool would win the club's first League and FA Cup double, beating arch-rivals Everton at Wembley to confirm the historic prize.

The following year, transfers were once again reasonably modest, reflecting the strength of the squad in place. Full-back Barry Venison arrived from Sunderland for £250,000; Steve Staunton was a snip from Dundalk at £50,000. Alan Irvine arrived from Falkirk for £75,000, and a tough local striker who had been playing amateur football for Waterloo Dock, John Durnin, took the massive leap from local obscurity to get his first step on the professional ladder.

Surprisingly, 1986/87 failed to deliver any silverware for Liverpool. "The whole crux was that we were not good enough," Kenny said. It was time to plot his first major rebuilding exercise.

Kenny was immediately supported from the top at Anfield. He said: "Ian Rush had gone to Juventus for £3.2m and Peter Robinson told me that we had some money to spend.

"Peter asked who we would like to bring in and I gave him five names. We ended up getting four of them (John Aldridge came from Oxford in January 1987 for £750,000; Nigel Spackman arrived in the February from Chelsea for £400,000; John Barnes joined from Watford in the June for £900,000; Peter Beardsley followed in the July from Newcastle for £1.9m).

Kenny said: "People like Peter Robinson were fantastic at doing their job when it came to transfers. If we were half decent at our bit, we gave ourselves a chance.

"We had a great mix of players. It was unusual for Liverpool to have two or three new players coming straight into the first-team from the start of the season. Normally people went into the reserves and had to work their way in.

For those new lads to settle so quickly was a great credit to them."

The excitement among the fans was remarkable. Kenny had not just made signings. He had bought skill and vision. A great squad had become an exceptional group. He said: "It was really enjoyable for everyone and a joy to go to work. The boys really enjoyed playing in front of the fans, so it was happy days for everyone."

Liverpool would win their 17th championship with a Rolls Royce quality that impressed the whole of football. Kenny said: "You look back at some of the special goals we scored. I remember John Barnes' great goal at Anfield in a 4-0 win against QPR. Digger made a great run from the halfway line, waltzing past two defenders before slotting the ball into

INSTANT HIT: John Barnes made a huge impact after arriving from Watford, while Nigel Spackman (above) also landed himself a championship medal

VIEW FROM THE DUGOUT: Kenny was more manager than player in '87/88

'IT WAS A GREAT DRESSING ROOM, FULL OF SO MANY TREMENDOUS CHARACTERS – NOT THAT I WAS ALLOWED IN!'

the Kop net. Then there was Peter Beardsley's goal against Arsenal when he nutmegged Michael Thomas and chipped goalkeeper John Lukic."

John Aldridge also scored his 20th goal of the season in that 2-0 win.

But back to the opening question. Just how good was that team that included the likes of Bruce Grobbelaar, Alan Hansen, Mark Lawrenson, Gary Gillespie, Stevie Nicol, Ronnie Whelan, Ray Houghton, Craig Johnston, and Gary Ablett, plus the stars already mentioned? It was such a great side, that Kenny only managed two league appearances himself that season! But then he had another focus which was about striving every day to maintain Liverpool's dominance of the English game.

He said: "A question like that is for the people who have watched and enjoyed all the great Liverpool teams. They can decide. I have not seen every Liverpool team. I played in some great ones myself.

"But it was a very good team. Ray Houghton came in during October 1987 which also helped us. He was a smashing, intelligent footballer. He had played with Aldo at Oxford and that also helped."

As Kenny smiles and adds: "It was a really good dressing room – not that I was allowed in! When I entered, the conversation stopped! To be successful you need a great dressing room and it was very unusual to have so many tremendous characters in one squad."

By then, of course, Kenny was concentrating on his

THE ONE THAT WE WANT: Bruce Grobbelaar and John Aldridge get their hands on the championship trophy

managerial role. So what did he enjoy more, playing or planning things from the Anfield hot seat? He said: "There is nothing better than being a player when everyone is in form and you have great team-mates.

"Everyone says that the best part of your football career is playing and enjoying the banter. But it's equally good being a manager. I can't say I prefer one role over the other. As a player you have to prepare yourself for every game. As a manager, you have to prepare the team. It's just different responsibilities, but being a manager at Liverpool should always include a complete understanding and humility about what has gone before.

"All the truly great Liverpool teams had one thing in common. Yes, they had a lot of outstanding players. The attitude was always right and everyone showed total commitment. But there was a humility and modesty about winning things and a desire to go out and do it again the following season.

"If we won a trophy, I always remember the backroom staff like Ronnie Moran would say things like 'Well, I suppose we've got a job next week!'

"We are the latter day beneficiaries of that type of Liverpool FC mindset. Nothing was taken for granted. Everything had been done in exactly the same way since 1959 when Shanks first came in. Big stars would be signed, but they would fully understand that they would have to conform to Liverpool Football Club, never the other way round. That is what makes the club so special."

Kenny Dalglish will forever be remembered for always putting Liverpool FC first.

When it comes to his wonderful 87/88 championship team, it can be said for him. They were very special indeed, a dream team to watch every Saturday. Better than the Brazilians? Let's just say they would have given any global club or international side an awful lot to think about any day of the week. They were world class.

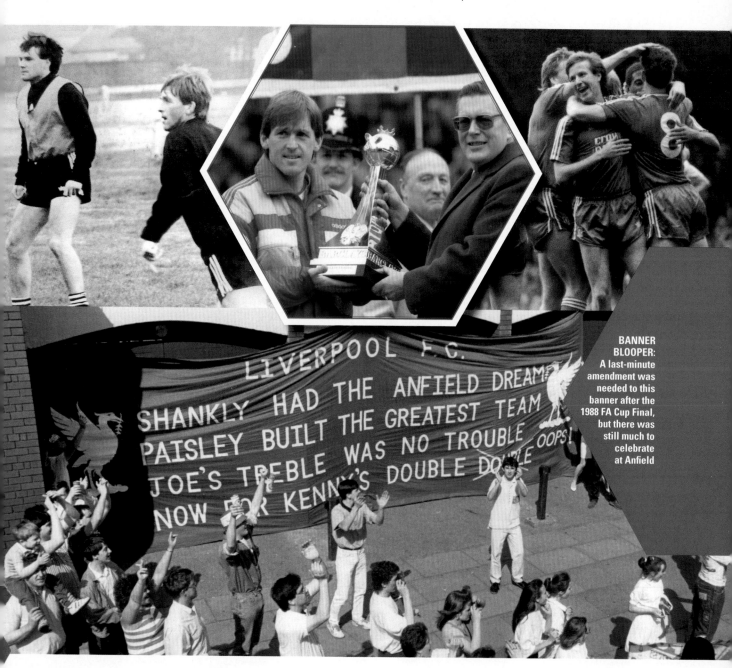

BANNER BLOOPER: A last-minute amendment was needed to this banner after the 1988 FA Cup Final, but there was still much to celebrate at Anfield

SWEET REVENGE

A 2-0 derby victory lay down a title marker and more than made up for the Reds' only defeat so far as the Anfield men reached the table's summit – a position they wouldn't relinquish all season

IF a team is tested more in defeat than in victory then Kenny Dalglish was given plenty to be happy about in November.

The Everton loss in the Littlewoods Cup could have derailed the Reds' season, could have hurt their confidence, could have damaged their self-belief.

It did the opposite.

A swift revenge victory over Everton saw the month get off to a flyer and Dalglish, beaming in front of the BBC cameras, was given all the assurance he would ever need that his side could go the distance this term.

November saw several important milestones. Liverpool's draw with Wimbledon in their rearranged fixture meant the Reds had achieved their greatest ever start to a league campaign – 10 wins and two draws – and the later 4-0 win over Watford saw Liverpool return to the top spot. And stay there for the rest of the season.

Not every Red was happy though. Jan Molby's stop-start season continued when he injured his ankle in a reserve match as he tried to fight his way back to fitness following a pre-season broken foot.

In most normal seasons the loss of 'Rambo' would have been dreadful but by November Liverpool were clicking so well that Dalglish had no concerns about there being a void in creativity - players were queueing up to entertain.

November also saw the House of Commons trying to muscle in on the success of Liverpool and others. A crazy idea from a group of MPs to dock Liverpool points for their summer spending spree was met with widespread derision.

It's safe to say that these ideas were proposed from the comfort of Westminster. The reception if they had been launched at Anfield may have been less respectful...

Back in the real world, Liverpool finished the month on top, on fire and on their game.

The last match of November was played at White Hart Lane but Terry Venables' arrival as manager of Tottenham Hotspur could not change their fortunes. Liverpool's journey to the ground might have been delayed because of heavy traffic but they were far too fast for anything the London side could come up with.

Barclays Football League
Division One
Sunday, November 1
Anfield

Liverpool 2
McMahon 35, Beardsley 70

Everton 0

PETER BEARDSLEY, the most expensive of Kenny Dalglish's new signings, finally earned Anfield acceptance with his stunning goal in the 2-0 victory over Everton.

The England striker had found himself overshadowed thus far by the magic of John Barnes and the reliable finishing of John Aldridge.

But he couldn't have picked a more important moment to demonstrate why Kenny Dalglish paid £1.9m for his services.

"It was nice to score in a derby," said the modest Beardsley, who admitted the pressure was building up on him at Anfield.

"It was bound to happen – it's all because of the fee. But it is no problem. If I wasn't doing the business I wouldn't be in the side," he said.

"People build you up and when things don't go perfectly they try to knock you down again but if the manager is happy then so am I."

Beardsley struck the ball in off the underside of the crossbar in the 70th minute after Steve McMahon had put Liverpool on the way to revenge for their midweek Littlewoods Cup defeat by their neighbours with a coolly-taken 35th-minute strike.

In the passion of Anfield's second derby in four days, it was difficult to disentangle the wider implications of the victory.

McMahon admitted afterwards: "It was a frantic game but we knew we had to win this one to save a bit of pride for ourselves and the supporters.

"Everton turned us over on Wednesday but I think we got our own back today. They overpowered us then, they showed 110 per cent commitment but we were confident we wouldn't let them do it again."

Liverpool were now two points clear at the top with games in hand and were ready to stretch out into the distance by carrying on picking up results in virtually every match.

Liverpool: Grobbelaar, Gillespie, Lawrenson, Nicol, Whelan, Hansen, Beardsley, Aldridge, Johnston, Barnes, McMahon.
Everton: Southall, Stevens, van den Hauwe, Ratcliffe, Watson, Reid, Steven, Clarke (Mountfield), Sharp, Snodin, Wilson.

Attendance: 44,760

Uncut fact:
The attendance of 44,760 was the second highest at Anfield in 1987, only bettered by the 44,827 attending the Merseyside derby in May.

Barclays Football League
Division One
Wednesday, November 4
Plough Lane

Wimbledon 1
Fairweather 78

Liverpool 1
Houghton 62

v Tottenham Hotspur

WIMBLEDON fought back to earn a draw at Plough Lane after Kenny Dalglish's side looked on course for another victory.

Ray Houghton's first Liverpool goal after a mazy run put the Reds 1-0 up, but Carlton Fairweather scored a late equaliser to ensure the points were shared.

It wouldn't be the last time the Dons proved to be a thorn in Liverpool's side.

Wimbledon: Beasant, Goodyear, Bedford, Thorn, Gayle, Fairweather, Gannon (Cork), Sanchez, Ryan, Gibson (Hazel), Fashanu.
Liverpool: Grobbelaar, Gillespie, Lawrenson, Nicol, Whelan, Hansen, Beardsley, Aldridge, Johnston (Houghton 62), Barnes, McMahon.

Attendance: 13,454

Uncut fact:
Ray Houghton netted his first Liverpool goal while this draw made it the Reds' best ever start to a league campaign, surpassing the opening 10 results in 1961 and 1978.

v Watford

Barclays Football League
Division One
Sunday, November 15
Old Trafford

Manchester United 1
Whiteside 49

Liverpool 1
Aldridge 21

LIVERPOOL left Old Trafford with a point after an enthralling clash with Manchester United.

John Aldridge was on target – yet again – for the Reds to give Dalglish's side the lead, but Norman Whiteside's second-half equaliser wasn't unexpected as Alex Ferguson's men had poured forward throughout the game looking for a result.

Man United: Walsh, Anderson, Gibson, Duxbury, Blackmore, Moran (Davenport), Robson, Strachan, McClair, Whiteside, Olsen.
Liverpool: Grobbelaar, Gillespie, Lawrenson, Nicol, Whelan, Hansen, Beardsley, Aldridge, Johnston, Barnes, McMahon.

Attendance: 47,106

Uncut fact:
Steve McMahon's yellow card for a foul on Bryan Robson was only the second booking received by any player so far this season.

Barclays Football League
Division One
Saturday, November 21
Anfield

Liverpool 0

Norwich City 0

A RARE goalless afternoon meant Liverpool drew their third consecutive game.

John Aldridge missed three gilt-edged opportunities, but the visitors – aided and abetted by a superb display from goalkeeper Bryan Gunn – were in no mood to concede and happily left Merseyside with a point.

Liverpool: Grobbelaar, Gillespie, Lawrenson, Nicol, Whelan, Hansen, Beardsley (Johnston 65), Aldridge, Houghton, Barnes, McMahon.
Norwich: Gunn, Brown, Elliott, Bruce, Phelan, Butterworth, Crook, Drinkell, Rosario, Putney, Gordon.

Attendance: 37,446

Uncut fact:
Norwich became the first side to stop Liverpool scoring in the league, allowing Arsenal to take over at the top of the table.

v Tottenham Hotspur

Barclays Football League
Division One
Tuesday, November 24
Anfield

Liverpool 4
McMahon 54, Houghton 64, Aldridge 68, Barnes 71

Watford 0

THE Reds returned to their goalscoring ways as they comfortably thrashed Watford at Anfield.

After failing to break down Norwich in their previous match, Kenny's team reminded the rest of the league that they meant business this season.

Steve McMahon, Ray Houghton, John Aldridge and former Watford star John Barnes all netted in the second half.

Liverpool: Grobbelaar, Gillespie (Spackman 79), Lawrenson, Nicol, Whelan, Hansen, Beardsley, Aldridge (Walsh 79), Houghton, Barnes, McMahon.
Watford: Coton, Chivers, Morris, McClelland, Jackett, Blissett, Sherwood (Rostron), Porter, Hodges, Allen, Senior (Sterling).

Attendance: 32,396

Uncut fact:
Kenny Dalglish's men went back to the top of the table after this 4-0 win – and stayed there for the rest of the season.

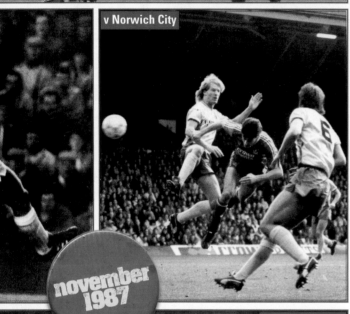

v Norwich City

november 1987

v Norwich City

Barclays Football League
Division One
Saturday, November 28
White Hart Lane

Tottenham Hotspur 0

Liverpool 2
McMahon 63, Johnston 80

STEVE Hodge's early dismissal opened the door for Liverpool to earn an important victory over Spurs at White Hart Lane.

The England international was sent off after 17 minutes for elbowing Ray Houghton in the face and Liverpool finally made their extra man pay towards the end as Steve McMahon and Craig Johnston secured the three points.

Tottenham: Parks, Hughton (Claesen 68), Thomas, Ruddock (O'Shea 73), Fairclough, Mabbutt, C Allen, P Allen, Waddle, Hodge, Stevens.
Liverpool: Grobbelaar, Gillespie (Spackman 86), Lawrenson, Nicol, Whelan, Hansen, Walsh (Johnston 68), Aldridge, Houghton, Barnes, McMahon.

Attendance: 47,362

Uncut fact:
Liverpool's team bus was delayed in the London traffic en route to White Hart Lane, forcing Kenny Dalglish to give his team talk far later than planned.

v Manchester United

THEY TALK DEAD FUNNY, BUT THEY PLAY DEAD GREAT...

MY SOUND AS A POUND '87/88 TEAM-MATES, BY JOHN ALDRIDGE

BRUCE GROBBELAAR

Bruce was eccentric. Everything you've probably heard about Bruce was right. He was a loveable, likeable character, although I think he exaggerated a few stories about his time in the jungle with the army and all that! On the serious side, he was a very good goalkeeper. If he ever made a mistake he would rectify it and in the dressing room he was very focused before games. He used to do this thing where he would volley the ball at the dressing room light switch until he knocked the light off. It used to drive us all f*****g mad! Sometimes he'd be the last one out for the warm-up and claim he'd just done it and we'd be thinking 'yeh right,' but that was Bruce. He was a really great character.

MIKE HOOPER

Hoops was a big lad. I got on with him really well. If you ever went out for a drink with Hoops you could never match him. He was unbelievable. I remember my first Christmas party at Liverpool and he called me over to the bar: 'Aldo, watch this'. He lined up seven pints of lager and necked the lot of them in under a minute. He's the only man I've ever seen do that and by the end of the night he was in better condition than me! I'll tell you what as well, I wouldn't have liked a haymaker from Hoops. He was a strong lad, not the most agile, but whenever he stepped in he did well. There was a game at Stoke in the FA Cup when he had to play and he kept a clean sheet to keep us in it. Goalies never got rotated back then so if he was playing now he'd have got games in the cups. He was a bit unlucky in that sense and in that Bruce very rarely got injured.

GARY GILLESPIE

There were a lot of different characters in the dressing room and Gary was a lad who would chip in even though he was one of the quieter players. He'd always join in socially. If we were out, he'd be out to have a bevvy with the lads. He was a solid defender and he got some important goals for us. He got the winner at Luton, at home to Sheffield Wednesday and goals against Nottingham Forest and Man United that season. Gary was good from corners – a great header of the ball – and I think he and Alan Hansen would be ideal centre-halves in today's game. They both read the game so well that they didn't have to mix it or lunge in. When I was at Oxford, the two centre-halves – Shotton and Briggs – defended by battering people. Gary was totally different to that. He could read situations and was good on the ground. In five-a-sides at training, Gary and Jocky were as good as anyone with the ball.

We went to Coventry in the second game of the season with Steve Nicol scoring two. We got a penalty and I said 'Nico, here you go, get your hat-trick'. Hansen wasn't having it. He told Nicol to 'f**k off' and said to me 'you're the penalty taker. This game isn't won so stick the ball in the net.' I did as I was told and slotted it past Steve Ogrizovic. When Jocky needed to be a captain, he would be one

ALAN HANSEN

At the time, Jocky was probably the best centre-half in the game. He was like a Beckenbauer. Well, a poor man's Beckenbauer! Seriously, Alan was fantastic. Brilliant on the ball and so good in the five-a-sides you'd think he was a midfield playmaker. He had an elegance about him. Jocky was the captain of the side but to be honest I think anyone of us could've skippered that team. He very rarely had to step in to do anything. We went to Coventry in the second game of the season and were 2-0 up with Steve Nicol scoring two. We got a penalty and I said 'Nico, here you go, get your hat-trick'. Hansen wasn't having it. He told Nicol to 'f**k off'

and said to me 'you're the penalty taker. This game isn't won so stick the ball in the net.' I did as I was told and slotted it past Steve Ogrizovic. That put us 3-0 up and we won 4-1. It was good captaincy, very professional. There was another game the following season when we got beaten 4-1 at West Ham in the League Cup and he responded to that by taking us all out the following day and getting us bladdered! He came in and said 'lads, we're having a dog day.' It was brilliant. When he needed to be a captain, he would be one. I know people talk about him maybe being a manager, but while he was very knowledgeable about football he suffered from terrible nerves before games. He'd be on the toilet all the time. People saw him on the pitch and thought he was unflappable, but before the game he was s******g himself. You'd never guess it though from the way he played. I played against him for both Oxford against Liverpool and Ireland against Scotland and I have to say he read the game brilliantly.

MARK LAWRENSON

When I joined Liverpool, Lawro was struggling with injury and was towards the end of his career. I think I'm right in saying he got injured when we beat Arsenal at Anfield and never played again, which was awful to see as he was only something like 30 at the time, not much older than me. I also played with Lawro for Ireland and he was another defender who could play in midfield. I remember us beating Scotland 1-0 at Hampden Park and I laid the winning goal on for him. It tells you everything about Lawro that he could play so well both at the back and in midfield. He wasn't underrated among professional footballers, but maybe the fans took him for granted. Again, Lawro read the game brilliantly and was a great tackler. That was the best part of his game. If there was a last-ditch challenge to be made, he would make it.

STEVE NICOL

Nico was another great lad to have in the dressing room, a really popular character. He took plenty of stick from the lads, but what a player he was. Versatile, quick and equally as good at right-back and left-back, he also had a phenomenal goalscoring record for a full-back. We went up to Newcastle quite early in the season for a game that was on the telly. They had Mirandinha, a Brazilian striker, making his debut and the focus was also on Peter Beardsley making his return to St James' Park. Nico stole the show. He scored a hat-trick playing down the right. How many full-backs can you think of who have scored hat-tricks? I think he had another one disallowed too and if Jocky hadn't stopped him taking that penalty at Coventry he would've had two hat-tricks to his name by mid-September. He'd be worth a lot of money in the game today would Nico.

BARRY VENISON

Venners thought he was the trend setter, but he wore some mad gear. Him and Barnesie were as bad as each other. A fella called Billy, a good friends of ours, used to get us all the top clobber from Versace for cost price in exchange for tickets. Most of us would get the sensible gear, the Versace or Boss stuff, but Venners would get some absolutely ridiculous clobber. I think Barry and Barnesie were having a competition to see who'd stand out the most. Again, Venners was a good player. Very little got past him and he had a fantastic ping on him. I used to show for the right-back and spin off. There was a goal at Charlton I remember particularly well from the following season when he pinged a fantastic ball into the corner of the 18-yard box that I scored from. Venners rarely lost the ball and he knew how to defend. He was probably the least highlighted player – apart from his hair of course! – in the team, but he always did his job.

GARY ABLETT

Abbo did his apprenticeship at Liverpool and the coaches knew he was going to make it. He broke into the first-team at left-back, then right-back and ended up at centre-back. Wherever he played, Abbo was solid. In his early days he got caught out once or twice, but that happens to most young players. He got better and better as he got older. Abbo was a really good friend of mine. We used to live in houses that were back-to-back to each other so we'd go in to training together. I know Gary spoke of being a little over-awed at being in the dressing room when he first broke through into the team and that was because he was a Liverpool fan. He went from cleaning the boots of his heroes to sitting next to them while someone cleaned his boots. I was the same when I first went to Liverpool. I'd grown up standing on the Kop and there I was playing in front of it. Abbo was a very honest

lad, a nice fella and it is very hard for me to think that he's no longer here. To lose him at such a young age was such a shame.

ALEX WATSON

I got quite friendly with Alex. He was very similar to his brother Dave – exactly the same stature and they both played at centre-half. He made his debut that season, down at QPR I think, but he was very young at the time and only just coming through. I know the coaching staff had high hopes for him and he was still at Liverpool when I left, but for whatever reason it didn't work out for him. To be fair, it must have been very hard to try and follow in the footsteps of Hansen, Gillespie, Lawrenson and Ablett.

RONNIE WHELAN

I played with 'Vitch' many times for Liverpool and Ireland and all I can say is that he was an absolutely fantastic player. I think he was called 'Vitch' because of the way he said 'which', but he already had the nickname when I got to Liverpool. He used to get a bit of stick from the crowd, which I could never understand, because he was very reliable. Ronnie was the quiet assassin in that Liverpool

*Ronnie was the quiet assassin in that Liverpool team. When someone needed to get hit – and in those days you could get away with it – Ronnie was the man who would hit them. People don't realise that when someone needed putting in their place, Ronnie would put them in their f*****g place! He got goals, too, big goals for both Liverpool and Ireland*

team. When someone needed to get hit – and in those days you could get away with it – Ronnie was the man who would hit them. He learnt a lot from Jimmy Case and Graeme Souness, the best people in the game at doing it. People don't realise that when someone needed putting in their place, Ronnie would put them in their f*****g place! He got goals, too, big goals for both Liverpool and Ireland and he captained us in the FA Cup final the following season against Everton because Jocky was injured. Ronnie was brought up playing with Kenny and Jocky. He was close to them, listened to them and learnt from them.

JAN MOLBY

The lads called him Janbo, which came from Rambo, and although he missed most of this season with injury he was the best passer of the ball I've played with. To be honest, I wasn't a good trainer, but at least I ran around a bit at Melwood! Jan would just stand there, get the ball and ping it on a sixpence here, there and everywhere to whoever was on his team. His passing range was phenomenal. The only Liverpool players I've ever seen come close to Jan for passing are Stevie G and Xabi Alonso. What a shot Jan had on him too. People say he wasn't mobile, but he was within his own reach. He was a clever player and his footwork was frightening. He'd get the ball, use it and never give it away. His long-range passing was brilliant. Jan would've thrived in the modern game because of the sports science. We used to drink like fish and Jan sometimes ate the wrong things,

but can you imagine how good he would've been in the modern game with sports scientists, nutritionists and all the rest working with him? You're talking a proper player. Another Alonso. A fella who could play anywhere – Real Madrid, Barcelona, wherever. He'd have been perfect for the modern game. Don't forget, we had to play on muddy, uneven pitches a lot of the time and got a lot of kicks from behind that went unpunished. Anyone who says a player like Jan would never have made it in the modern game is talking rubbish.

NIGEL SPACKMAN

I used to room with Nigel or Ray Houghton so we became really pally. He was a great lad – a quirky Cockney. Kenny bought him when Ian Snodin's move to Liverpool broke down. Snods was supposed to sign for Liverpool on the same day I did, but he went to Everton instead so Kenny bought Spackers from Chelsea. He didn't let anyone down when he played, he was a super player. He'd run all day for the team, had loads of energy, was a good passer of the ball and could tackle. Because Ronnie Whelan and Steve McMahon had forged such a great midfield partnership when Jan got injured, Spackers didn't get as many games as he'd have liked, but he still played 33 times that season and slotted in when called upon. That said, it was easy to slot into that Liverpool team. The system was easy to adapt to and the balance was phenomenal – possibly the best Liverpool have ever had.

STEVE MCMAHON

Steve McMahon sure can rap! Macca mixed it when he had to. He put his foot in when it was needed. People talk about the Vinnie Jones tackle on him at the start of the FA Cup final winning the game for Wimbledon. What a load of bollocks. Losing momentum before the game having won the league with games to spare was the biggest problem. Macca was a Billy Bremner-type midfielder. An old school central midfielder who could tackle, pass the ball and score goals. He scored some brilliant long-range goals because of the shot he had on him. The one at home to Man United stands out. The one thing that truly epitomised Steve McMahon, though, was my tap-in against Arsenal at Anfield. You won't see better skill, desire and determination than when he kept the ball in on the touchline, used the advertising board to push himself back onto the pitch and skipped past a flying challenge to pass the ball to Peter Beardsley who teed me up. That's how Steve was – passionate for Liverpool. He came from a family of Evertonians, supported and played for them himself, but you'd never have known it for a second when he had a Liverpool shirt on.

RAY HOUGHTON

I think Kenny decided to sign both me and Ray after seeing Scotland play against Ireland. We'd already clicked playing together at Oxford and had an almost telepathic understanding so he thought that he'd put us together towards the right of the pitch and get Barnes and Beardsley to combine towards the left. Before Ray, Kenny had Craig Johnston on the right and with all due respect to him – because Cruggy was a fine player – he was all pace and played with his head down. Ray was a very, very intelligent player. He had a football brain and was always switched on. He knew what was in front of him, who was behind him and where the space was to pass into. Ray was a better player than Craig and he enhanced the team when he arrived from Oxford that October. He was a creative player, but also one who scored goals including the FA Cup winner at Everton. I was lucky enough to play nearly all my games for Oxford, Liverpool and Ireland alongside Ray so I know how good he was. He was a special player – but a right know-it-all! He loved going to quizzes and he knew absolutely everything. I'm telling you, he'd argue with our Lord if he thought he was right. That's the way he was. He now works in the media and he

Macca was a Billy Bremner-type midfielder. An old school central midfielder who could tackle, pass the ball and score goals. He scored some brilliant long-range goals because of the shot he had on him. He came from a family of Evertonians, supported and played for them himself, but you'd never have known it for a second when he had a Liverpool shirt on

is very, very good at it because, all joking apart, he knows football. He's an intelligent, football-minded man and he's the one player from this team that I'm surprised didn't go into management. He could've been a great manager or coach, but then he was clever enough to realise that he could earn a living working for RTE and others, just like Jocky has done from the BBC, so why make life harder for yourself if you don't have to? It's for the same reason that I walked out of management.

JOHN BARNES

The best player I have ever played alongside. Simple as that. He was unmarkable. You ask Jan Molby, who played with Johan Cruyff at Ajax, who the best player he's ever played with is. He'll say 'John Barnes.' Barnesie was the best player in our team. Everyone loved him and his ability to beat a man was unbelievable. I used to get the ball down, give it to him and get into the box because I knew a quality cross was guaranteed to come in. He knew whereabouts I would be in the box and had the ability to put the ball into an area for me to attack it. He'd go past players like they weren't there and the 1988 FA Cup semi-final against Nottingham Forest sticks in my mind. Before the game, Forest right-back Steve Chettle had said he was going to have 'Barnes on toast' and it was all over the papers. I got onto it. I started taking the piss out of him because I knew it would wind him up. I was saying 'Chettle has got you toast today Barnesie, you won't see the ball'. It wound him up big time and for the first hour of that game he absolutely ripped Steve Chettle. He was mega; absolutely sensational. I scored both goals, the first a penalty after Chettle had brought him down and the second a volley after a perfect Barnes cross. And, just to rub it in four days later, he took the piss out of Chettle again when we beat Forest 5-0 at Anfield, although, to be fair to the lad, very few right-backs could keep Barnesie at bay. It's just a pity he never got to play in the European Cup for Liverpool. John won PFA Player of the Year and Football Writers Footballer of the Year and – this is purely hypothetical – had we been playing in Europe at the time then with him in that kind of form we'd have got very far in the European Cup. AC Milan had a very good side, but we'd have challenged them and Barnesie would've had his name in lights all over the world. He could've walked into that AC Milan team no problem. People criticised him for his England career, but England were a very ordinary side in the late 1980s. We weren't.

CRAIG JOHNSTON

Craig was mad as a hatter. A good lad, but his mind was always ticking over. He'd come up with all kinds of ideas – such as inventing the mini-bars you now get in hotels – and he wrote the Anfield Rap. He was a bright lad, but lived his life at 100mph. What you saw on the pitch was how he was off it. He was a good footballer, Craig, and did a lot of damage down the right with his pace. He lost his place to Ray and then retired at the end of that season when he was only 27 to return to Australia to look after his ill sister.

JOHN WARK

Jink was a great character. I was really friendly with John. Even to this day we get on really well. He'd come down to Garston and have a bevvy with us every now and again on a Sunday and if there was a charity night he'd always be there. He left Liverpool during the season after only playing a few games, but what a great midfield goalscorer he was. His strike-rate for Liverpool, Ipswich and Scotland was phenomenal because he was a great finisher. After we'd both left Liverpool, I remember him marking me during a Tranmere v Ipswich game at Prenton Park. I didn't get a kick. Not one. We got beat 1-0 and he was brilliant. I was gutted because I wanted to get one over on him and I thought I'd have an easy night because he was an attacking midfielder playing at centre-back. When we play our Liverpool legends games now he still plays at centre-half because he reads the game so well. Mentally, he was very strong and physically he was strong as well, but he is such a likeable fella. He never said anything bad about anyone and I was sorry to see him leave Liverpool that year.

KEVIN MACDONALD

Kevin had a bad injury at Liverpool – a broken leg – and only recovered in time to play one game that season. Because of that I didn't see an awful lot of him on the pitch, but when he returned to training I could see he was a good player. Some players come back from bad injuries with no problems, but some are never the same and Kevin was one of them. Something similar happened to Jim Beglin. How could Kevin have got back into one of the most flamboyant Liverpool sides of all time anyway after over a year out? If you got injured or suspended it was very, very difficult to get back in.

PETER BEARDSLEY

Peter was very quiet. Really, really quiet and very focused on playing football. He loved playing for Liverpool, but loved playing for England just as much. Peter cost £1.9m that summer, a lot of money, but it was an astute piece of business. Liverpool had proper scouts then and a manager who knew the players. Peter was a magnificent player to play with. His footwork was ingenious. Some of the goals he scored, the way he could skip past a man, was not too dissimilar to Luis Suarez or even Kenny. The goal that he scored at home to Arsenal, when he nutmegged Michael Thomas and then chipped the ball over John Lukic was superb. When you look at that team, we basically played a 4-4-1-1 with Peter dropping off behind me, like Kenny used to drop off behind Rushie. Liverpool were the first English team to play that way. When I was pushing the centre-halves back, Peter was sat in the hole picking up loose balls and shuffling it out to Barnesie. Ray used to go mad because Peter always looked to his left first. He'd call him all kinds of things and say he was only passing it to Barnesie because he wanted to play for England with him! I'd balance that out by always looking for Ray on my right foot when I turned, but Peter was the reason that Barnesie got so much of the ball. Defenders didn't know how to deal with him. If they faced up to him he could play it through to me, if they backed off he'd run with the ball at them. If you look at a lot of the goals from that season you'll see me crossing over from one side to the other to take defenders away. That allowed Peter to run at his man and only have to skip past one player to score a goal. The four

of us – me, Peter, Ray and Barnesie – all had football brains. I was fortunate in that movement came naturally to me. I knew how to move defenders into areas that they didn't want to be in, but if they didn't come with me the other three had the ability to play me in. That's how we clicked as a four – we were ridiculously good. The other thing about Peter was that he didn't feel the pressure in wearing the number seven shirt. Maybe the shirt number wasn't highlighted as much as it is now because people talk about Suarez being the first to fill the seven shirt since Keegan – who I loved – Kenny and Peter Beardsley. They're the three prominent number sevens. Since then only Steve McManaman and now Suarez have got near to being in the same category.

> *Peter cost £1.9m that summer, a lot of money, but it was an astute piece of business. Liverpool had proper scouts then and a manager who knew the players. Peter was a magnificent player to play with. His footwork was ingenious. Some of the goals he scored, the way he could skip past a man, was not too dissimilar to Luis Suarez or even Kenny*

PAUL WALSH

Walshy lost out when Peter Beardsley was signed. The money Liverpool spent on me, Peter, Ray and Barnesie was unfortunate for him because he had great skill, but he wanted to play so it was understandable that he left. In the modern day, he'd have stayed at Liverpool and been rotated with Peter and myself or used from the bench a lot more. Paul is a cracking lad and I'm still good friends with him now. He used to buzz about the place and had a lot of natural ability. I remember Nike coming to Liverpool to do a big magazine promo. We went to Anfield after training and a photographer stood on the pitch and said 'go on Walshy, show me what you can do'. Walshy started doing keepy-ups. He was flicking the ball up doing all kinds of tricks while this fella was snapping away. Next he says 'right Aldo, let's have the same from you'. I got the ball ran down towards the Annie Road end and smashed it into the net. I said 'that's me done,' and walked off! There was no way I was following Walshy!

KENNY DALGLISH

Kenny was brilliant to play for, a great manager. When I first came to Liverpool in January 1987 I hardly played. I was usually sub and only now and again did I get to start. I found it really frustrating having played in every game for Oxford in the First Division before moving to Liverpool. I just wanted to play football and I wasn't getting any younger. To be honest, I was pissed off, but Kenny pulled me to one side one day and said 'I'm not playing you because we play through the middle to Rushie. When Rushie goes, we're going to play out wide and get the balls in for you. It'll all work out for you, just be patient and trust me.' I did trust him and that's exactly what happened in 1987/88 – but then he brought Rushie back! Kenny was a good man-manager, but very rarely did he need to do team talks because we were such a good side. Kenny brought some fantastic players to Liverpool. He created a superb team and he was able to see that he could gel four new attacking players – me, Barnesie, Peter and Ray – very quickly because we were gifted internationals who could perform on the big stage. He got the blend right in that team and that's why we played such flamboyant football. We were all British and Irish lads who knew how to play in the First Division from our times at Oxford, Watford and Newcastle, whereas these days trying to blend some of the continental players in can be a lot harder. It really was great management to put the four of us together and both Kenny and Ron Yeats – Liverpool's chief scout at the time – need applauding for that.

JOHN ALDRIDGE

You might not know this, but the lads used to call me 'Stonkers'. That was the word I'd use instead of 'bollocks' and it stuck. Even now if Kenny, Jocky or Nico phone me they'll be like 'alright Stonks' when I answer. I got the Golden Boot that year but it's only recently that I realised that I actually scored 26 league goals. Quite a few of them were pens, but you've still got to stick them in. I set a new club record at the start of the season by scoring in each of the first nine games and if you add my goal at Chelsea on the final day of the previous season then I scored in 10 consecutive league games. Ruud van Nistelrooy is the only other player to have done that in the top division and because all his goals came in the same season, whereas one of mine was in the previous campaign, I think it gets forgotten that I share the record. I'd waited 28 years to wear a Liverpool shirt and I was determined to prove myself. I knew I was a good goalscorer and there was no way I was going to let the opportunity to score goals for the club I love slip through my fingers. My aim was to stay in that Liverpool shirt for as long as I could. I scored 63 goals in 104 appearances. There's not a lot more I could've done. My strike ratio at Liverpool was a goal every 1.65 games and of all the Liverpool strikers to have played 100 games or more I think only Gordon Hodgson has a better record. I'm very proud of that. All I wanted to do was play for Liverpool. I loved the club when I was six and love the club now that I'm almost 56. I've got three grandkids now and one of them, Jamie, who is seven, is just starting to realise that I played for Liverpool. The thought of being able to have a pint with him when I'm older and say 'this is what I achieved, I lived the dream' makes me extremely proud. To be second in the all-time Liverpool goalscoring ratio list above some of the great names to have played for our club is something I'd like to be remembered for. If they put 'second best goalscoring ratio for Liverpool' on my tombstone I'd be made up!

John Aldridge was speaking to CHRIS McLOUGHLIN

REDS SHORT ON GENEROSITY

Festive spirit may have been high on the agenda throughout most of the country, but Kenny's men were in no mood to hand any gifts to their opponents as the gap at the top started to widen

THE Pet Shop Boys' "Always On My Mind" kept The Pogues' "Fairytale of New York" off the Christmas No.1 spot but there was no doubt who was top of the first division charts with the Reds looking ever more dangerous.

There were only five games in December but Liverpool continued to prosper as they won four of these and drew the other. They scored 12 goals in the process and conceded just three. Clearly, Liverpool were in no mood to spread any festive goodwill.

December 1987 also saw a significant contract extension at Anfield for a man who had never made a single appearance for the club but whose role at Liverpool became the byword for calm, measured and intelligent leadership.

General secretary and chief executive Peter Robinson never set the Kop alight with a header, never saved a penalty, never lifted a single piece of silverware but his behind-the-scenes stewardship of Liverpool, beginning in 1965, had helped lead the club to where it was in 1987. Nobody wanted that to end so a near eight-year extension was added to his deal.

Kevin MacDonald left the club to return to Leicester City on loan as he continued to try and recover from a long-standing leg injury and he was unlikely to feature in Dalglish's plans for the rest of the year.

Barry Venison was a happier injury story as he returned to the first-team after achilles trouble in the 1-0 victory over Sheffield Wednesday.

The bookies by now were so confident – or scared – of Liverpool going the season entirely unbeaten that they dropped the odds of it happening to 14-1. You know you're on to something when the bookmakers are starting to run for the hills – the same place that every other team in the division were heading.

The month ended with a dramatic and brilliant annihilation of Newcastle United. Four goals that could have been eight and an overall Liverpool performance littered with individual and collective genius.

What a way to sign off 1987.

Could 1988 start in the same manner? Could the year ahead be full of even more highlights?

What do you think?

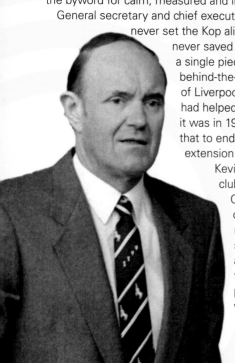

LIVERPOOL *The Anfield Review 60p*

Barclays Football League
Division One
Tuesday, December 28
Anfield

Liverpool 4
McMahon 4, Aldridge 48pen, 76, Houghton 88

Newcastle United 0

JOIN the club – Liverpool Football Club that is – and every day will seem like Christmas, every game will resemble a cup final.

That's the way it was when Newcastle visited. The Reds were not so much counting the people locked in Anfield, as the unfortunates locked out. Football was booming at the home of the undisputed championship favourites and it was easy to see why.

The equation is simple. Entertainment, skill, passion and total commitment – in that order – equals bumper crowds that were the envy of the country. The gates were shut 50 minutes before kick-off with Newcastle United standing between the Merseysiders and an unbeaten record stretching back 20 games.

It was a good day to compare the much-publicised golden boy of Tyneside, Mirandinha, with a certain John Barnes. Barnes was willing to work for the side, tackle back and take knocks in the thick of the action. Mirandinha was a goal-hanger and never turned out to be a great in the English game because of that.

He could have scored twice in the second half but was foiled by Bruce Grobbelaar before Liverpool took control.

Steve McMahon crashed home the opener and once the Reds finally clicked into gear John Aldridge won a soft penalty that he then converted.

At 2-0 the game was over as a contest and Kenny Dalglish's men added further finishes from Aldridge and Ray Houghton to send Newcastle back to the north-east with nothing to show for their Christmas efforts.

Liverpool kept reminding us that the championship is a marathon. If that's the case, why had they been sprinting from the word go without a pause for breath?

There may still have been plenty of time left in the season but the Reds had to be comfortable title favourites after a performance like this.

Liverpool: Grobbelaar, Gillespie, Venison, Nicol, Whelan (Spackman 81), Hansen, Beardsley, Aldridge, Houghton, Barnes (Johnston 81), McMahon.
Newcastle: Kelly, McDonald, Wharton, McCreery, Anderson, Roeder, D Jackson (Bogie), Gascoigne, Goddard, Mirandinha, Cornwell.

Attendance: 44,637

Uncut fact:
Liverpool's third goal in this 4-0 win was their 50th of the season in the first division, an outstanding record after 21 games.

STORY OF THE MONTH

v Chelsea

Barclays Football League
Division One
Sunday, December 6
Anfield

Liverpool 2
Aldridge 67pen, McMahon 87

Chelsea 1
Durie 22pen

STEVE McMahon's late winner ruined Chelsea's hopes of leaving Anfield with a point.

John Aldridge's second-half penalty for Liverpool cancelled out Gordon Durie's own first-half spot-kick before McMahon grabbed the win with three minutes remaining in a game the Reds had dominated from start to finish.

Liverpool: Grobbelaar, Gillespie, Lawrenson, Nicol, Whelan, Hansen, Beardsley, Aldridge (Johnston 86), Houghton, Barnes, McMahon.
Chelsea: Freestone, Clarke, Dorigo, Pates, McLaughlin, Wood, Nevin, Murphy, Dixon, Durie, Wilson.

Attendance: 31,211

Uncut fact:
The day after this win, Liverpool chairman John Smith announced that club secretary Peter Robinson had signed a contract extension to keep him at Anfield until 1995 by when he would have completed 30 years of service.

Barclays Football League
Division One
Saturday, December 12
The Dell

Southampton 2
Clarke 44, Townsend 71

Liverpool 2
Barnes 11, 38

THE Reds squandered a two-goal lead as Southampton refused to surrender at The Dell.

Liverpool seemed destined to win this match after a brace from John Barnes, but Colin Clarke pulled one back for the home side just before the break and Andy Townsend grabbed the equaliser 20 minutes from time.

Southampton: Burridge, Forrest, Statham, Moore, Bond, Cockerill, Townsend, Case, Baker (Le Tissier 80), Clarke (R Wallace 80), D Wallace.
Liverpool: Grobbelaar, Gillespie, Lawrenson (Ablett 19), Nicol, Whelan, Hansen, Beardsley, Aldridge, Houghton, Barnes, McMahon.

Attendance: 19,507

Uncut fact:
Gary Ablett made his first appearance of the season after Mark Lawrenson limped off with a hamstring injury.

v Southampton

DELL EXIT: Mark Lawrenson limps off at Southampton

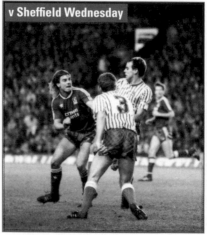

v Sheffield Wednesday

O EXIT

Barclays Football League
Division One
Saturday, December 19
Anfield

Liverpool 1
Gillespie 76

Sheffield Wednesday 0

GARY Gillespie's winner 14 minutes from time helped Liverpool to a narrow victory against the Owls.

Wednesday arrived at Anfield hoping for a point and nothing more with their super-defensive set-up meaning the Reds struggled to break them down.

However, The Kop breathed a sigh of relief towards the end as Gillespie finally broke the deadlock, side-footing home to secure the victory.

Liverpool: Grobbelaar, Gillespie, Venison, Nicol, Whelan, Hansen, Beardsley (Johnston 70), Aldridge, Houghton, Barnes, McMahon.
Sheff Wed: Hodge, Sterland, Worthington, Madden, Pearson, Proctor, Chamberlain (May), Owen (West), Chapman, Megson, Marwood.

Attendance: 35,383

Uncut fact:
Liverpool's win extended their unbeaten league run from the start of the season to 19 games, equalling the club's top-flight record set in 1949/50.

LEAVING IT LATE: Steve McMahon celebrates an 87th-minute winner against Chelsea

december 1987

ONLY GOAL: Gary Gillespie's strike sinks the Owls

Barclays Football League
Division One
Saturday, December 26
Manor Ground

Oxford United 0

Liverpool 3
Aldridge 42, Barnes 54, McMahon 61

OXFORD old boys John Aldridge and Ray Houghton returned to the Manor Ground and helped Liverpool to a comfortable win.

Aldridge scored Liverpool's first – a close range finish – before John Barnes and Steve McMahon added gloss to the scoreline after the break.

Oxford: Hucker, Bardsley, Dreyer, Shelton, Hill (Mustoe), Caton, Hebberd, Whitehurst, Saunders, Phillips, Rhodes-Brown.
Liverpool: Grobbelaar, Gillespie, Venison, Nicol, Whelan, Hansen, Beardsley, Aldridge, Houghton, Barnes (Johnston 80), McMahon (Spackman 80).

Attendance: 13,680

Uncut fact:
John Aldridge netted on his return to his former club as Liverpool established a 10-point lead at the top of the table due to Arsenal's defeat to Nottingham Forest.

45

The programme has always been a big part of the match day experience for Reds fans. The Anfield Review in the 1987/88 season is memorable and unique - just like the team. Here we take a look through some of the features Reds were reading throughout the campaign...

KENNY'S COLUMN:

Come on, admit it, who's got this tracksuit in the loft somewhere at home? King Kenny rocking the classic trackie in his must-read manager's notes. No better way to get a programme started than by hearing what the great man thinks. CCTV is clearly all the rage back then too.

QUIZ TIME:

The game is 20 minutes away, you're safely in place and watching the clock. What better way to wind down the time until kick-off than with the Anfield programme 'Soccer Quiz'. And if you didn't now the answers at least you could entertain yourselves with snaps of Peter Beardsley and Steve Nicol doing what they did best.

CUP-FINAL day ... and King George VI meets Liddell as the Liverpool players line up before Arsenal.

HEROES FOR HEROES:

Nice swing Alan. Although the Kop may have vibrated every week to the sound of thousands cheering their heroes, don't forget that every Liverpool player also had their own inspirations. Alan Hansen is a big fan of Jack Nicklaus, Pele and his fellow countryman Denis Law. Great choices by a great player.

PEN PALS:
Fuming at something? Smiling at something else? Then pick up a pen and tell the programme about it. We may live in days where interaction with fans is done via Twitter and the club website but back in 1987/88 good old pen and paper was the best way to tell the club what you thought.

UNSUNG HEROES:
It's good to see Anfield's unsung heroes (or heroines in this case) getting a mention in the programme.

TRAVEL CLUB:
Are you "Going Places"? Why not do so with the Anfield Travel Club? For example, you can get to Plough Lane to watch the Reds against Wimbledon and back for £8.50. A bargain (especially as Ray Houghton scored a brilliant mazy dribble).

SHOP AROUND:
Looking for that hard-to-find birthday present? Fancy yourself as an amateur architect? If so, buy the self-assembly model of Anfield, just £4.95. They're on sale now at the souvenir shop...

MINE'S A PINT:
It's no secret that quite a few fans like a pint before going to the match. Back in 1987/88 you could combine your love of the Reds and beer by drinking 'Super Reds Premium Lager.' It was "Super Special!" for a "Super Team!"

CLASSIC KOP:
The Kop had been out of action at the start of the season due to emergency repairs. But this photo shows the old place in all its glory. Some serious old-skool moustaches going on there as well...

january 1988

POWERING INTO THE NEW YEAR

The Reds started 1988 as they'd finished the previous year – with another unbeaten month. This one included the start of an FA Cup campaign that would ultimately lead to Wembley

A NEW year. But the same old Liverpool.

After finishing 1987 with a 4-0 drubbing of Newcastle United, what better way to open 1988 than by putting another four goals past an equally hapless opponent?

Comic Relief might have just been launched by Rowan Atkinson but no Coventry City fans were smiling as they felt the wrath of the Reds. That meant Liverpool had now scored eight times past the Sky Blues in just two encounters.

That match was Liverpool's fourth clean sheet in a row and by the end of the day Liverpool had a 13-point lead at the top of the table.

One player who wouldn't be staying at Anfield to bask in the season's glory was midfielder John Wark. The Scotsman made 108 appearances for the Reds, scoring 42 goals, including 27 goals in the 1984/85 season – one more than the great Ian Rush – but his Anfield adventure was over as he decided to return to Ipswich Town.

The only slight blip January brought was the goalless FA Cup game against Stoke City at the Victoria Ground. Football was a different game back then played on what looks like a completely different surface.

The Stoke pitch that night would not be considered good enough for growing potatoes these days but Liverpool escaped the Potteries with a hard-fought draw before advancing without any further concerns in the replay.

January also saw the announcement of the end of one iconic shirt and the start of another. Crown Paints – who had sponsored Liverpool for six years – were to be replaced in 1988/89 with Candy in a three-year deal worth £1 million.

The last match of the month saw Bruce Grobbelaar recalled to the side at the expense of Mike Hooper. Grobbelaar had been injured earlier in January in training after being caught by a Steve McMahon challenge. Hooper had come in and done extremely well for three matches but Grobbelaar was always Dalglish's No.1 and he came back in for the victory over Aston Villa. It was as if he had never been away. Liverpool – with or without their first choice goalkeeper – were playing the kind of football that meant no side stood a real chance of stopping them.

CANDY GAIN: Some of the Reds' stars in the new Candy strip several months before they started wearing it in action

Barclays Football League
Division One
Saturday, January 16
Anfield

Liverpool 2
Aldridge 44, Beardsley 61

Arsenal 0

EUROPEANS among the 250 million televiewers who watched Peter Beardsley, John Barnes and company demolish Arsenal found out just what they had been missing since Liverpool were banned from playing competitive matches abroad.

Although this was by no means one of their best performances, the sheer quality of the two goals scored by Beardsley and John Aldridge will live in the memory of many for a long time.

They were compelling moments of brilliance of a kind that is rarely seen anywhere, and only become possible when a side possesses individuals of genuine international ability.

Beardsley's goal in the 60th minute, chipped cheekily over goalkeeper John Lukic's head after a marvellous, stuttering run past three defenders, rightly dominated Sunday's headlines but it was Aldridge's score on the stroke of half-time that really decided the match and symbolised Liverpool's irresistible spirit.

John Barnes' flowing run down the left wing and in along the byeline to the goalmouth had the Kop rising in salute of a certain goal but somehow the Arsenal defence scrambled the ball away.

The ball rolled towards touch, but was unexpectedly retrieved by Steve McMahon whose desperate exertions sent him flying into the crowd, before he passed the ball on to the lurking Beardsley.

Lukic got down well to save his shot, only to find Aldridge following up to chalk up his 20th goal of the season.

To do them justice Arsenal did put up a brave fight and held their own for much of the match.

But Liverpool had become used to dominating sides and there was no way they were going to let the Gunners back into the contest.

And even though the Reds had played better than this during their sensational run so far, the three points were duly delivered by a side that looks ever more comfortable in its own skin.

Liverpool: Hooper, Gillespie, Lawrenson (Spackman 51), Nicol, Whelan, Hansen, Beardsley, Aldridge, Houghton, Barnes, McMahon.
Arsenal: Lukic, Winterburn, Sansom, Williams, Caeser (Thomas 46), Adams (Groves 77), Rocastle, Hayes, Smith, Quinn, Richardson.

Attendance: 44,294

Uncut fact:
This game was shown live on television around the world, attracting an estimated 250m viewers and Michel Platini to Anfield as a pundit for French TV.

Barclays Football League
Division One
Friday, January 1
Anfield

Liverpool 4
*Beardsley 22, 83, Aldridge 53,
Houghton 75*

Coventry City 0

THE Reds went on the rampage for a second successive match as they thrashed Coventry City 4-0.

Just 72 hours after beating Newcastle United by the same margin, Kenny Dalglish's men again showed why they are the in-form team of the season.

A brace from Peter Beardsley plus goals for John Aldridge and Ray Houghton ensured Coventry had a terrible start to 1988.

Liverpool: Grobbelaar, Gillespie, Venison (Ablett 51), Nicol, Whelan, Hansen, Beardsley, Aldridge, Houghton, Barnes, McMahon (Spackman 87).
Coventry: Ogrizovic, Borrows, Kilcline, Smith, Downs, Bennett (Livingstone), McGrath, Phillips, Gynn (Rodger), Regis, Speedie.

Attendance: 38,790

Uncut fact:
The Reds scored four goals for the eighth time in their opening 22 league games to begin 1988 13 points clear of second-placed Nottingham Forest.

v Coventry City

FA Cup
third round
Saturday, January 9
Victoria Ground

Stoke City 0

Liverpool 0

HOPES of a comfortable passage into the FA Cup fourth round were hit after a goalless draw at the Victoria Ground.

In a tight contest, Stoke should have earned a late shock when Graham Shaw ran through on goal but Mike Hooper brilliantly read the situation and blocked the young substitute's effort to force a replay.

Stoke: Barrett, Dixon, Carr, Bould, Berry, Ford, Parkin, Talbot, Henry, Stainrod (Shaw 75), Morgan.
Liverpool: Hooper, Gillespie, Lawrenson, Nicol, Whelan, Hansen, Beardsley, Aldridge, Houghton, Barnes, McMahon.

Attendance: 31,979

Uncut fact:
Mike Hooper appeared for the first time this season in place of the injured Bruce Grobbelaar as Division Two Stoke became the first side to stop Liverpool scoring away from home.

FA Cup
third round replay
Tuesday, January 12
Anfield

Liverpool 1
Beardsley 9

Stoke City 0

LIVERPOOL had to fight hard to beat Stoke City and advance to the FA Cup fourth round.

Although the Reds created 15 chances, with John Barnes and Ray Houghton playing on the opposite wings to normal in a tactical change, Peter Beardsley's mis-hit shot after nine minutes proved to be the only goal of the game.

Liverpool: Hooper, Gillespie, Lawrenson, Nicol, Whelan, Hansen, Beardsley, Aldridge, Houghton (Johnston 82), Barnes, McMahon.
Stoke: Barrett, Dixon, Carr, Talbot, Bould, Berry, Ford, Henry, Morgan, Stainrod, Parkin (Shaw).

Attendance: 39,147

Uncut fact:
Peter Beardsley scored his first FA Cup goal for the Reds and in doing so became the first Liverpool player to score in the competition since Ian Rush in the 1986 final victory over Everton at Wembley.

BEARDSLEY BRACE: Two goals from our number seven helped the Reds to their eighth four-goal haul of the season – this time against Coventry City

arlton Athletic

AT IT AGAIN: Beardsley nets against Charlton

v Aston Villa

WHITE STUFF: A rare outing for the white shirt, but a familiar result as John Barnes helped the Reds to a cup win at Villa

january 1988

Barclays Football League
Division One
Saturday, January 23
Selhurst Park

Charlton 0

Liverpool 2
Beardsley 30, Barnes 60

LIVERPOOL made it 24 unbeaten league games with an easy victory over Lennie Lawrence's Charlton outfit at Selhurst Park.

Peter Beardsley gave the Reds the lead as he mopped up a rebound following a John Barnes effort before Barnes himself made it 2-0 after the interval with a right-footed effort.

The victory put Liverpool 17 points clear at the top of the First Division.

Charlton: Bolder, Humphrey, Reid, Shirtliff, Thompson, Bennett (Gritt 62), Mortimer (Crooks 65), McKenzie, Campbell, Jones, Lee.
Liverpool: Hooper, Gillespie, Venison (Spackman 84), Nicol, Whelan, Hansen, Beardsley, Aldridge (Johnston 74), Houghton, Barnes, McMahon.

Attendance: 28,095

Uncut fact:
Such was the interest in seeing Liverpool that Charlton attracted their biggest home attendance since 1980.

FA Cup
fourth round
Sunday, January 31
Villa Park

Aston Villa 0

Liverpool 2
Barnes 53, Beardsley 86

ANOTHER 2-0 win and another goal apiece for John Barnes and Peter Beardsley. The duo had both netted in the game before against Charlton in the league and they repeated their double act here – but in reverse.

Barnes opened the scoring shortly after the interval with a fine header before Beardsley secured Liverpool's passage into the fifth round with a second just four minutes from time.

Aston Villa: Spink, Gage, Gallacher, Gray, Evans, Keown, Birch, Lillis, Thompson, Daley (Aspinall), McInally.
Liverpool: Grobbelaar, Ablett, Venison, Nicol, Spackman, Hansen, Beardsley, Aldridge, Houghton, Barnes, McMahon.

Attendance: 46,324

Uncut fact:
Bruce Grobbelaar returned from injury as Liverpool kept a club record ninth consecutive clean sheet.

51

february 1988

KENNY'S THE PRIZE GUY

Accolades, honours and the birth of his fourth child made February another momentous month for the King as his team powered on in the league and knocked their Mersey rivals out of the FA Cup

AS Eddie 'The Eagle' Edwards did his best to represent Great Britain at the Winter Olympics, news arrived from north of the border that Kenny Dalglish had just as many fans in Scotland as he had on Merseyside.

After representing Scotland 102 times, he was awarded the title of 'Scottish Honour Player' along with anyone else who had featured more than 50 times for Scotland.

February continued to get better for Dalglish as he was also awarded the Bells Manager of the Month Award before the West Ham United game – even if Liverpool followed that up with a listless performance that belied their reputation as the most lethal side in the land.

There were more comings and goings on and off the pitch at Anfield as well as Paul Walsh joined Tottenham Hotspur in a £500,000 deal while Kenny and wife Marina celebrated the birth of Lauren – the couple's fourth child.

Jan Molby also ended his injury nightmare when he came on for Steve McMahon in the win over Watford. The Dane had not played a single senior minute up to that point in the season due to his foot and ankle problems and he was determined to make up for lost time – if Liverpool needed him to.

The brutal truth for Molby was the first XI had done so well without him that the calls for his immediate return were not exactly deafening. The month's biggest fixture was undoubtedly the FA Cup fifth round win over Everton at Goodison Park. Ray Houghton, who had already done enough to justify his transfer fee from Oxford United, scored the first headed goal of his career to beat Liverpool's close rivals and ensure Merseyside bragging rights went to the red half of the city.

As the month ended, the Reds got a short respite from the English cold and the demands of the season as they headed to Spain to prepare for Sammy Lee's testimonial. Most of the rest of Division One were hoping Liverpool got stuck on the Continent. Permanently.

FA Cup
fifth round
Sunday, February 21
Goodison Park

Everton 0
Liverpool 1
Houghton 76

A MOMENT of brilliant combination play between the terrific trio of Peter Beardsley, John Barnes and Ray Houghton enabled Liverpool to continue their relentless pursuit of their second league and FA Cup double in three years at Everton's expense.

There were plenty of critics ready to accuse Kenny Dalglish of wasteful extravagance when he paid £2.8 million for Barnes and Beardsley, and then a further £800,000 for Houghton in mid-season, but this was another example of the triumvirate's true worth.

Genuine stars are so rare they are worth their weight in gold – and they proved it again.

In a match so defensively orientated that neither side managed a serious shot or a corner in the first half, it needed something special to break that deadlock.

And that was exactly what happened in the 75th minute when Beardsley played the perfect return pass behind Gary Stevens for Barnes, the winger curled a teasing cross just out of Neville Southall's reach and Houghton dived to head the winner on his first derby appearance.

Although none were consistently outstanding, each one had the ability to turn a match in a split-second, as was the case here. Quality will always shine through eventually and it was that rare quality that attracted Dalglish to them in the first place.

Now that both Everton and Manchester United were out of the reckoning for the FA Cup, Dalglish's men were considered serious contenders for another double. Few would have bet against them.

Everton: Southall, Stevens, Pointon, van den Hauwe, Watson, Reid (Bracewell), Steven, Heath, Sharp, Snodin, Power (Harper).
Liverpool: Grobbelaar, Ablett, Venison, Nicol, Spackman, Hansen, Beardsley, Aldridge, Houghton, Barnes, McMahon.

Attendance: 48,270

Uncut fact:
Kenny Dalglish celebrated the birth of his daughter Lauren by leading Liverpool to their first FA Cup win at Goodison Park since 1955.

STORY OF THE MONTH

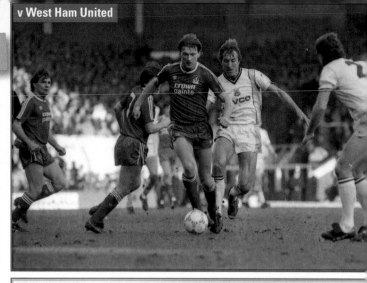

v West Ham United

Barclays Football League
Division One
Saturday, February 6
Anfield

Liverpool 0

West Ham 0

WEST Ham held Liverpool to a draw for the second time that season with a dour draw at Anfield.

The visitors' ambitions stretched no further than trying to keep a clean sheet and they managed that with aplomb as Liverpool repeatedly failed to break them down in what was generally a disappointing and lacklustre game.

Liverpool: Grobbelaar, Ablett, Venison, Nicol, Spackman, Hansen, Beardsley, Aldridge (Johnston 77), Houghton, Barnes, McMahon.
West Ham: McAllister, Stewart, Ince, Bonds, Strodder, Gale, Ward, Brady, Dickens (McQueen), Cottee, Robson.

Attendance: 42,049

Uncut fact:
Before kick-off, Kenny Dalglish was presented with the Bells Whisky manager of the month award for January, the third time this season he had received it.

v Watford

Barclays Football League
Division One
Saturday, February 13
Vicarage Road

Watford 1
Blissett 75

Liverpool 4
Beardsley 29, 49, Aldridge 47, Barnes 60

LIVERPOOL found their scoring boots again as they comfortably beat Watford at Vicarage Road.

For the second time this season, the Reds scored four against the Hornets as a Peter Beardsley brace, plus further strikes from John Aldridge and John Barnes, ensured the three points.

Watford: Coton, Gibbs, Morris, McClelland, Rostron, Jackett, Sherwood, Porter, Sterling, Allen, Senior.
Liverpool: Grobbelaar, Ablett, Venison, Nicol, Spackman, Hansen, Beardsley, Aldridge, Houghton, Barnes (Johnston 79), McMahon (Molby 79).

Attendance: 23,838

Uncut fact:
Luther Blissett's goal was the first the Reds had conceded in 1988 while on the Monday following this game Paul Walsh was sold to Tottenham for £500,000.

Barclays Football League
Division One
Saturday, February 27
Fratton Park

Portsmouth 0

Liverpool 2
Barnes 49, 85

A JOHN Barnes double ended Portsmouth's 10-game unbeaten run but it wasn't one of the Reds' best displays of the season.

Barnes opened the scoring just after the break with a deflected effort off defender Billy Gilbert before stroking home his second just five minutes from time.

Portsmouth: Knight, Gilbert, Sandford, Dillon (Hardyman 74), Blake, Ball, Horne, Fillery, Quinn, Connor, Hilaire.
Liverpool: Grobbelaar, Ablett, Venison, Nicol, Spackman, Hansen, Beardsley, Aldridge, Houghton, Barnes, McMahon.

Attendance: 28,117

Uncut fact:
Pompey boss Alan Ball said afterwards: "Liverpool play my type of football. If you have to get beaten, it's nice to enjoy it. I enjoyed watching that today."

february 1988

v Portsmouth

PERFECT PETER: Peter Beardsley steers home one of two goals against the Hornets

55

KEN ROGERS

A SIMPLE PHILOSOPHY MADE THE REDS GREAT VIEWING FOR THE FANS AND THE LIVERPOOL ECHO'S FOOTBALL CORRESPONDENT IN THE 1980s

PLEASURE TO WATCH: John Aldridge celebrates a goal against Coventry with the masses in the Kop

Back in the 1980s, I used to wake up every morning and thank the football gods that I had the best job in the world.

I was the football correspondent for the Liverpool ECHO with the highly unusual task of covering Liverpool FC one month and Everton FC the next. And just in case you have forgotten, this was the greatest decade in the history of Merseyside football for winning silverware.

Between both clubs they won:

8 league titles (6 to Liverpool).
3 FA Cups (2 to Liverpool).
4 League Cups (all to LFC).
2 European Cups (Liverpool building further on the glory of the Seventies).
1 Cup Winners Cup (Everton's single Euro trophy).

That's 18 major trophies in a silver-laden Merseyside decade.

I know sports journalists who have never been to an FA

PLENTY TO REPORT: Ken Rogers on duty at Anfield

Cup Final, let alone reported year in, year out on glorious title-winning seasons. And so I sailed through the Eighties on the crest of a wave of success that is unique in the history of English football.

During that period, I worked closely with Messrs Paisley, Fagan and Dalglish. Each fashioned their teams in the image of what had gone before; in other words the football gospel according to Bill Shankly. Each slightly modified the Rolls Royce engine that was Liverpool FC at that time.

To be honest, while I'm aware that there is a school of thought that Kenny's 1987/88 title winning team was the best of the lot - 'Better than the Brazilians' - I would personally find it extremely hard to separate the very special teams of those great managers. For instance, in 1988 Kenny himself only figured in two league games, masterminding another championship win from the touchline.

And I would argue that in naming Liverpool's greatest side, he would have to be in it. Then I immediately think about Ian Rush, Graeme Souness, Ray Clemence, Ray Kennedy, Jan Molby, Terry McDermott, Phil Thompson and so on – all greats who played in 80s teams – and I further question whether you can pinpoint one team over another.

But what I have absolutely no doubt about is that Liverpool created a way of playing during this period that was almost hypnotic. Opponents were mesmerised as soon as their coach drove through the Shankly Gates. They were further doubting themselves as they walked under the 'This Is Anfield' sign, and by the time they actually got out on the pitch they were looking up at the standing Kop with its swaying mass of Scouse testosterone with one simple thought in their heads: 11 against 20,011 isn't very good odds.

And then the Anfield Road, the Main Stand and the Kemlyn Road would decide to have a say. The one thing that I always felt at this time was that Liverpool seemed to have twice as many players on the pitch as their opponents. The Boot Room mentality about pass and move, preferably forward and not sideways, and total support for a team-mate every time he received the ball meant that Liverpool players always appeared to have two or three options, while the opposition only seemed to have one option – and that was to defend for their lives.

I wrote the autobiography of a player who was a giant in the previous decade and so it was nothing new. Tommy Smith used to explain Liverpool tactics to me in the simple terms I can only assume came out of the mouths of Messrs

'TOMMY SMITH USED TO EXPLAIN LIVERPOOL TACTICS TO ME IN THE SIMPLE TERMS I CAN ONLY ASSUME CAME OUT OF THE MOUTHS OF MESSRS SHANKLY, FAGAN, PAISLEY, MORAN, AND THEN DALGLISH, ON A DAILY BASIS AND HAD NOTHING TO DO WITH COMPLICATED FLIP CHARTS AND RIDICULOUS TOUCHLINE INSTRUCTION CHARTS. IT WENT SOMETHING LIKE THIS: "SUPPORT YOUR MATES!"'

RARE APPEARANCE: Kenny Dalglish comes off the bench for John Aldridge

Shankly, Fagan, Paisley, Moran, and then Dalglish, on a daily basis and had nothing to do with complicated flip charts and ridiculous touchline instruction note books. It went something like this: "Support your mates!"

It all seems so ludicrously simple. Support your mates; respect everyone inside the bastion that is Anfield; assume the tea lady is always more important than that season's record signing; grasp immediately that no-one can ever be bigger than the club; pass and move; defend from the back; don't mess around with the ball in front of goal (or anywhere on the pitch); stick it in the back of the net.

There you have it, Jose Mourinho and the rest. The real 'special one' was an Anfield team talk in the 1980s that was probably about passing the liniment! I watch modern coaches taking what seems like an age to make a substitution and then showing a player on eighty grand a week a chart with a diagram of the pitch and where he should be standing.

I suspect the wise men of Anfield would have been saying: "If you don't know, you can't play!"

And so I smile when I think back to the Eighties when Liverpool were not just 'Better than the Brazilians' but on a football planet all of their very own.

Yes, Kenny's '87/88 team had all the attributes to play anybody off the park. The eccentricity of Grobbelaar; the versatility of Nicol; the calm control at the back of men like Hansen and Gillespie; the sheer magic and vision of Beardsley and Barnes; the local inspiration and goalscoring prowess of Aldo; the tackling strength and quality of McMahon; the class and eye for a crucial goal of Whelan; the dash and verve of Johnston – and so on.

And they also had that cry from somewhere deep down inside: "Help your mates!"

march 1988

HUMAN
AFTER ALL

A derby match in March saw the Reds taste their first league defeat as Lawro called time on his Anfield career but there was still plenty to cheer including the 10th four-goal haul of the campaign

SAMMY Lee's testimonial match – Osasuna v Liverpool – saw the Reds win 2-0 as Kenny graced the field and even managed to score himself. His presence on the pitch underlined his own admiration for the contribution Lee made to life at Liverpool – the archetypal 'local boy done good'.

While the match was played in the relaxed conditions of a testimonial, it did give Kevin MacDonald some important game time as his 18-month battle for fitness following a broken leg finally led to him featuring in the match.

The Reds' first league game of the month saw them defeat QPR at Loftus Road in a match where Alex Watson made his long-awaited debut in defence.

Later on in the FA Cup against Manchester City, Liverpool were a finely tuned, highly motivated machine, and it was a machine that trampled all over City as a 4-0 win underlined just how powerful Dalglish's side were.

The win was Liverpool's seventh consecutive away win, the 10th time they had scored four times in a game and their 24th clean sheet of the season. No wonder the league title seemed to be heading nowhere else but Anfield.

As the month progressed the statistics kept on coming including a 1-1 draw at Derby County that saw Liverpool draw level with Leeds United's record-breaking run in 1974 when they also went 29 consecutive games unbeaten from the start of the season.

The record seemed to be there for the taking but, unfortunately for the Reds, they fell at the final hurdle – and to Everton of all teams – in a 1-0 loss at Goodison Park.

More upsetting news came later in the month when the club announced the premature retirement of Mark Lawrenson, pictured here signing copies of his autobiography for fans in WH Smith, whose career was ended, aged just 30, by his ongoing achilles problem.

That put Liverpool's defeat into perspective and also gave Dalglish and his squad something to work for. To prove to 'Lawro' that the title would be theirs and theirs soon. It was the best tribute they could pay to a man who had excelled in his time at the club.

In the last match of a month in which Andy Gibb **(pictured above)** – brother of the Bee Gees – died at the age of 30, the Reds earned a 2-1 win against Wimbledon.

Dalglish even graced Anfield with his presence as he was a late substitute for John Aldridge.

Barclays Football League
Division One
Wednesday, March 16
Baseball Ground

Derby County 1
Forsyth 85

Liverpool 1
Johnston 54

THE STRAIN of chasing Leeds United's 14-year-old league record cost Liverpool two points at Derby in a match they could, and should, have won with ease.

Kenny Dalglish always maintained that his men were only interested in winning matches, not setting records, but it became painfully obvious that once Craig Johnston had put them in front after 53 minutes, they were content to try and protect their lead.

Ironically that safety-first approach, involving regular, untypical use of the back-pass to the goalkeeper, cost them dear in the end.

Derby, who had battled away with great courage and determination but little hope of scoring, seized the initiative and in one last desperate surge managed what only one other side had achieved in Liverpool's previous 15 games by scoring.

Left-back Michael Forsyth launched a determined raid down the left, substitute Gary Micklewhite fired a low cross into the goalmouth and Forsyth was there to do the near-impossible and beat Bruce Grobbelaar from close range.

So, although Liverpool had now made the best start to a First Division season by any club (they had won three more games than Leeds during their opening spell in 1973-74), they were left to bemoan their failure to win in style and distance themselves even further from all challengers.

Although they had tried commendably to concentrate on each game as it comes, they would hardly be human if all the fuss about Leeds' long-standing achievement had not got to them in the end.

It was now Dalglish's job to refocus his troops and ensure their return to winning ways.

Derby: Shilton, Blades, Forsyth, Williams, Wright, Hindmarch, McMinn (Micklewhite), Lewis (Garner), Gee, Gregory, Callaghan.
Liverpool: Grobbelaar, Gillespie, Ablett, Nicol, Spackman, Hansen, Beardsley, Johnston, Houghton, Barnes, McMahon (Molby 48).

Attendance: 26,356

Uncut fact:
Liverpool equalled Leeds United's 29-game unbeaten run from the start of a top-flight season record with this draw at Derby County.

59

STORY OF THE MONTH

Barclays Football League
Division One
Saturday, March 5
Loftus Road

QPR 0

Liverpool 1
Barnes 34

JOHN Barnes made it six goals in seven games as Liverpool edged past QPR on their artificial surface at Loftus Road despite being without John Aldridge.

The home side had most of the possession but they could not convert several great chances and Barnes punished them before half-time as he tapped in from close range to settle it after Craig Johnston's shot came back off keeper David Seaman.

QPR: Seaman, Dawes, Neill, Parker, McDonald, Maguire, Maddix, Falco, Byrne, Fereday, Kerslake.
Liverpool: Grobbelaar, Ablett, Watson, Nicol, Spackman, Hansen, Beardsley, Johnston, Houghton, Barnes, McMahon.

Attendance: 23,171

Uncut fact:
Alex Watson made his Liverpool debut while Kenny Dalglish named himself on the bench for the first time that season the day after his 37th birthday.

FA Cup
quarter-final
Sunday, March 13
Maine Road

Manchester City 0

Liverpool 4
Houghton 32, Beardsley 53pen, Johnston 77, Barnes 85

LIVERPOOL sealed their place in the FA Cup semi-finals with an exhibition against Manchester City.

It took Liverpool 30 minutes to break City down as Ray Houghton finally broke the deadlock before second-half goals from Peter Beardsley, Craig Johnston and John Barnes ensured City were well beaten at a soggy, muddy Maine Road.

Man City: Stowell, Gidman, Hinchcliffe, Brightwell, Lake, Redmond, White, Stewart, Varadi, McNab, Simpson.
Liverpool: Grobbelaar, Gillespie, Ablett, Nicol, Spackman, Hansen, Beardsley, Johnston, Houghton, Barnes, McMahon.

Attendance: 44,047

Uncut fact:
This was Liverpool's seventh straight away win and meant the Reds had reached the FA Cup semi-final without conceding a goal.

v QPR

v Manchester City

v Everton

v Wimbledon

march 1988

Barclays Football League
Division One
Sunday, March 20
Goodison Park

Everton 1
Clarke 14

Liverpool 0

WAYNE Clarke ended Liverpool's unbeaten run with the only goal of the Goodison derby.

Bruce Grobbelaar dropped a Trevor Steven corner into the path of Clarke who swept home in the 14th minute to settle it.

Ironically, Clarke's brother Allan was a member of the Leeds team of 1974 whose 29-game unbeaten record from the start of a season the Reds had equalled.

Everton: Southall, Stevens, Pointon, van den Hauwe, Watson, Reid, Steven, Clarke (Heath 78), Sharp, Harper, Sheedy (Power).
Liverpool: Grobbelaar, Gillespie, Ablett, Nicol, Spackman (Molby 82), Hansen, Beardsley, Johnston, Houghton, Barnes, McMahon.

Attendance: 44,162

Uncut fact:
Everton inflicted Liverpool's first league defeat of the campaign, ending their attempt to equal the 30-game unbeaten record set by Burnley during the 1920/21 season (although Burnley embarked on their run after losing their first three games of the season).

Barclays Football League
Division One
Saturday, March 26
Anfield

Liverpool 2
Aldridge 34, Barnes 76

Wimbledon 1
Young 88

LIVERPOOL bounced back from their first defeat of the campaign to beat a physical Wimbledon side 2-1.

John Aldridge and John Barnes scored for the home side and that was enough, despite Eric Young pulling one back two minutes before the end.

Liverpool: Grobbelaar, Gillespie, Ablett, Nicol, Spackman, Hansen, Beardsley, Aldridge (Dalglish 87), Johnston, Barnes, McMahon (Molby 72).
Wimbledon: Beasant, Scales, Phelan, Ryan, Young, Thorn, Cunningham, Cork (Sayer 81), Fashanu, Sanchez, Wise.

Attendance: 36,464

Uncut fact:
Jan Molby made his first Anfield appearance of the season and Kenny Dalglish appeared for the first time since May 1987.

BETTER THAN THE BRAZILIANS

A crucial trio of clashes against Nottingam Forest saw the Reds lose one, win an FA Cup semi-final, and then produce one of the most memorable performances in English football history

YOU **wait all season for one defeat and then two come along at once.**

After the loss at Everton in the penultimate game of March, Forest opened April with a 2-1 victory over Liverpool in the first of three matches the clubs would play against each other during the month. The match was Jan Molby's first start of the season but ended badly as the Reds failed to keep up their recent impressive form.

But Liverpool then shrugged that loss off as they tussled in a pulsating 3-3 encounter with Manchester United.

That return to form then continued and, just as Brendan Powell was riding Rhyme 'n' Reason to victory in the Grand National, Liverpool overcame Forest 2-1 to book a place against Wimbledon in the FA Cup final.

If Kenny Dalglish was hoisted onto the fans' shoulders after that victory then the reception that would have greeted him after the third Forest game four days later can barely be believed.

The red side of the city would have had Dalglish knighted on the spot as Liverpool subjected Brian Clough's side to the kind of footballing exhibition that only exists on computer games – and back in 1988 no Amstrad or Commodore could get close to being as fantastic as the team's performance that day.

It was the undoubted high point of what was a sensational season and will forever be remembered as the day Liverpool toyed with the opposition like never before.

Liverpool's league progress was then halted by a strange two-day event in London called the Football League Centenary Tournament which was set up to celebrate 100 years of league football in Britain.

Ironically enough, Forest won the event just days after Liverpool had destroyed them.

But as far as Kenny Dalglish was concerned they could keep that silverware – the only trophy he wanted was the league championship.

Fortunately for Dalglish and Liverpool's fans, the wait for league glory was brief. After a goalless draw with Norwich City, the Reds knew a victory over Tottenham Hotspur at home would be enough to wrestle the title back from the other side of Stanley Park.

Sure enough, a Peter Beardsley goal at 3.34pm on April 23, 1988 proved to be enough.

The title was back at Anfield. The plaudits did not end there either as the month ended with John Barnes winning the Football Writers Association's Footballer of the Year award. And who did he beat to that accolade? Team-mate Alan Hansen.

It truly was Liverpool's season.

GAME OF THE MONTH

Barclays Football League
Division One
Wednesday, April 13
Anfield

Liverpool 5
Houghton 18, Aldridge 37, 88,
Gillespie 58, Beardsley 79

Nottingham Forest 0

LIVERPOOL'S performance in defeating Nottingham Forest by five goals to nil at Anfield was so devastating that, at times, it seemed the two teams were playing different games.

It was the first time this season that Liverpool had scored more than four but the only wonder was that the total did not reach double figures, as it would have done without a remarkable goalkeeping display by Steve Sutton, a couple of equally remarkable misses by Ray Houghton and John Aldridge, and the intervention of both an upright and the crossbar.

Sutton gave the kind of display that Gordon Banks used to produce for Leicester in the Sixties.

He made at least a dozen saves, many from close range efforts that should have left him helpless, and only he knows how he kept out three tremendous shots from Peter Beardsley.

The least said about Forest's defence the better.

They fielded almost the same side that put up such a good fight in the FA Cup and although Des Walker aggravated his ankle injury early on – so badly that he had to be substituted at half-time – they should have been capable of giving the potential champions a thorough examination.

For most of the time it didn't seem to matter which player had the ball as Liverpool ran riot.

Ray Houghton opened the scoring after collecting a one-two from John Barnes before sliding home before John Aldridge sent Liverpool into the break 2-0 up as he linked up well with Peter Beardsley.

On the hour mark Gary Gillespie put the result beyond doubt with a close-range strike before further finishes from Beardsley and Aldridge ensured the rout was complete.

Even Ian Rush would have been pushed to gain a place in this astonishing team.

Liverpool: Grobbelaar, Gillespie, Ablett, Nicol, Spackman, Hansen, Beardsley, Aldridge, Houghton (Johnston 85), Barnes, McMahon (Molby 78).
Nottingham Forest: Sutton, Chettle, Pearce, Walker (Wassall), Foster, Wilson, Crosby, Webb, Clough, Glover, Rice.

Attendance: 39,535

Uncut fact:
Sir Tom Finney, watching in the Main Stand, said afterwards: "It was the finest exhibition I've seen in the whole time I've played and watched the game. You couldn't see it bettered anywhere, not even in Brazil. The moves they put together were fantastic."

START OF THE ROUT:
Ray Houghton prepares to put the Reds 1-0 up against Forest

Barclays Football League
Division One
Saturday, April 2
City Ground

Nottingham Forest 2
Hansen 24og, Webb 58

Liverpool 1
Aldridge 70pen

LIVERPOOL suffered their second First Division loss of the season as an Alan Hansen own goal and a Neil Webb strike proved to be enough to sink the Reds, with Jan Molby making his first start of the season.

John Aldridge scored a 70th-minute penalty to give Liverpool hope, particularly as Bruce Grobbelaar also saved a Nigel Clough spot-kick, but Forest hung on a week before the FA Cup semi-final.

Nottingham Forest: Sutton, Chettle, Pearce, Walker, Foster, Wilson, Crosby, Webb, Clough, Wilkinson, Rice.
Liverpool: Grobbelaar, Gillespie, Ablett, Nicol, Spackman, Hansen, Molby (Beardsley 57), Aldridge (Houghton 84), Johnston, Barnes, McMahon.

Attendance: 29,188

Uncut fact:
Bruce Grobbelaar saved a 47th-minute penalty from Nigel Clough, his first spot-kick save since denying Forest's Peter Davenport at the City Ground in 1985.

Barclays Football League
Division One
Monday, April 4
Anfield

Liverpool 3
Beardsley 38, Gillespie 41, McMahon 46

Manchester United 3
Robson 2, 59, Strachan 77

THE Reds squandered a 3-1 lead against 10-man Manchester United in a heated encounter at Anfield.

Goals from Peter Beardsley, Gary Gillespie and Steve McMahon cancelled out Bryan Robson's early opener for United before Colin Gibson was dismissed, but Robson got a second and Gordon Strachan scored an equaliser with 13 minutes to go.

Liverpool: Grobbelaar, Gillespie, Ablett, Nicol, Spackman, Hansen, Beardsley, Aldridge (Johnston 78), Houghton, Barnes, McMahon.
Manchester United: Turner, Anderson, Blackmore (Olsen), Bruce, McGrath, Duxbury (Whiteside), Robson, Strachan, McClair, Davenport, Gibson.

Attendance: 43,497

Uncut fact:
United boss Alex Ferguson later claimed refs are intimidated by the Anfield crowd, only for Kenny Dalglish, while clutching baby daughter Lauren, to interrupt and tell the interviewer: "You might as well talk to my daughter, you'll get more sense out of her."

FA Cup
semi-final
Saturday, April 9
Hillsborough

Liverpool 2
Aldridge 14pen, 51

Nottingham Forest 1
Clough 67

A SECOND double in three seasons was on as Liverpool booked a place in the FA Cup final thanks to a John Aldridge double at Hillsborough.

His first was a penalty after Steve Chettle fouled John Barnes and his second a brilliant volley. Nigel Clough pulled one back, but the Reds marched on to Wembley at Forest's expense.

Liverpool: Grobbelaar, Gillespie, Ablett, Nicol, Spackman, Hansen, Beardsley, Aldridge, Houghton, Barnes, McMahon.
Nottingham Forest: Sutton, Chettle, Pearce, Walker, Foster, Wilson, Crosby, Webb, Clough, Wilkinson, Rice.

Attendance: 51,627

Uncut fact:
The night after this FA Cup semi-final victory, John Barnes was voted PFA Player of the Year. Steve McMahon finished second, with Peter Beardsley third.

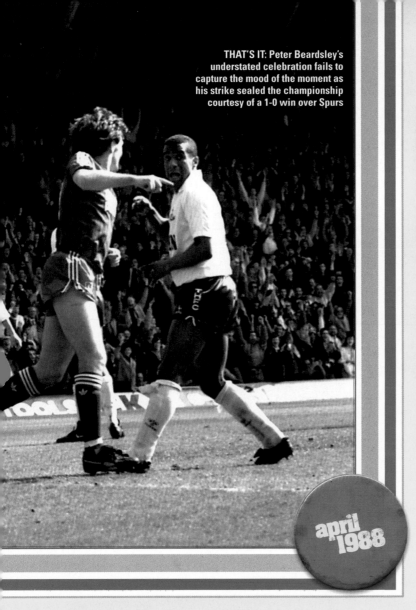

THAT'S IT: Peter Beardsley's understated celebration fails to capture the mood of the moment as his strike sealed the championship courtesy of a 1-0 win over Spurs

april 1988

Barclays Football League
Division One
Saturday, April 23
Anfield

Liverpool 1
Beardsley 34

Tottenham 0

PETER Beardsley was Liverpool's hero as his first-half finish secured the championship for the Reds.

His clinical strike clinched the title in style, much to the delight of Kenny Dalglish, who said afterwards: "No matter how many times you experience the thrill of winning the title that special tingle never diminishes. Seven members of our squad are sampling their first championship medals. I am sure they will want more."

Liverpool: Grobbelaar, Gillespie, Ablett, Nicol, Spackman, Hansen, Beardsley, Aldridge, Houghton, Johnston, McMahon.
Tottenham: Mimms, Statham, Thomas, Metgod (C Allen), Fairclough, Mabbutt, Walsh, P Allen, Waddle, Samways, Hodge.

Attendance: 44,798

Uncut fact:
Peter Beardsley's goal ensured Liverpool won a record 17th English league title with four First Division fixtures still to play.

Barclays Football League
Division One
Wednesday, April 20
Carrow Road

Norwich City 0

Liverpool 0

LIVERPOOL could not break Norwich City down as their attempts to be crowned champions were delayed by some inspired goalkeeping from Bryan Gunn.

Even so, the Reds would now have to lose their final five games, and see Man United win their last four while turning around a goal difference disadvantage of 32, to blow their championship hopes.

Norwich: Gunn, Culverhouse, Spearing, Linighan, Phelan, Butterworth, Fox, Drinkell, Fleck, Goss, Putney.
Liverpool: Grobbelaar, Gillespie, Ablett, Nicol, Spackman, Hansen, Beardsley, Aldridge, Houghton, Johnston, McMahon.

Attendance: 22,509

Uncut fact:
Norwich became the only side to prevent Liverpool scoring in either Division One match against them. Three points would have clinched the league title.

Barclays Football League
Division One
Saturday, April 30
Stamford Bridge

Chelsea 1
Durie 72pen

Liverpool 1
Barnes 75

JOHN Barnes scored a stunning free-kick from 30 yards out to earn a point at Stamford Bridge.

A Gordon Durie penalty gave the Blues the lead with just 18 minutes left, but Barnes produced a special goal, even by his standards, to equalise.

Chelsea: Hitchcock, Hall, Dorigo, Wicks, McLaughlin, Clarke, Hazard, Nevin, Dixon, Durie, Bumstead.
Liverpool: Grobbelaar, Watson, Whelan, Nicol, Spackman, Hansen, Johnston, Aldridge (Beardsley 76), Houghton, Barnes, McMahon.

Attendance: 35,625

Uncut fact:
Ahead of kick-off, John Barnes was announced as the Football Writers Association's Footballer of the Year with Alan Hansen in second place. LFC players received an astonishing 96% of the votes.

ON THE RAMPAGE: John Barnes was in scintillating form again as the Reds took high-flying Forest apart

LFC 5
FOREST 0

THE FLOODGATES ARE OPEN: Ray Houghton picks his way through the centre of the Nottingham Forest defence after a one-two with John Barnes to open the scoring

UNSEEN ACTION

'THAT IS ANOTHER SUPERB LIVERPOOL GOAL': The memorable commentary from John Motson said it all as John Aldridge made it 2-0 against Forest, but there was even more high quality football to come

IN ON THE ACT: Gary Gillespie hammers the ball in from close range at the Kop end to make it 3-0

FIVE-STAR PERFORMANCE: John Aldridge rounds off the scoring from close range after Nigel Spackman had cut the ball back to him

UNSEEN ACTION

LFC 5 FOREST 0

MESMERISING SKILL: John Barnes is congratulated for his spell-binding assist that allowed Peter Beardsley to stroke in the Reds' fourth

PETER HOOTON
THE LEAD SINGER OF THE FARM STOOD IN 'THE CROWN' ON WALTON ROAD ON THE NIGHT OF APRIL 13 1988 AND LOOKED AT HIS MATES IN STUNNED SILENCE

MIND-BLOWING FOOTBALL
Steve Nicol fires a shot goalward during a superb exhibition of football by the Reds in April 198[8]

'IN THE END WE USED TO STAND ON THE KOP WISHING THE OPPOSITION WOULD GO 2-0 UP SO WE COULD GET A GAME. WE JUST BELIEVED WE WOULD WIN 3-2 – THE ARROGANCE THAT COMES WITH SUCCESS I SUPPOSE. BUT WE WERE THAT GOOD WE JUST KNEW ANYTHING WAS POSSIBLE'

He should've been smiling and talking about Liverpool's performance earlier that evening. But he, along with most of the rest of the pub, couldn't quite believe what they had just seen.

He had walked down to the pub after witnessing that match against Nottingham Forest, the 5-0 demolition of a fine Brian Clough side that prompted national footballing treasure Sir Tom Finney to describe it as "the finest exhibition I've seen in the whole time I've played and watched the game. You couldn't see it bettered anywhere, not even in Brazil."

When Hooton thinks back to the game, and the whole 1987/88 season, it doesn't take long for him to sum up his feelings – and they're not far behind Sir Tom himself.

"Mind-blowing," he says with a grin. "We were mind-blowing that season. We played a style of football that we had never even dreamed about. I had been going the match for over 15 years by this point but we played in a style that I never thought was possible.

"When we beat Forest everyone in the pub was stunned. We didn't think we'd ever see anything like that again. Then we heard what Finney had said and we couldn't get over it. Finney – Shankly's mate – saying that about us.

"He'd seen the Hungarian side of the 50s, he'd seen all the great teams all over the world. And he put us in the same bracket. Everything Liverpool tried that night came off. Back-heels, flicks – everything Barnes and Beardsley attempted was brilliant. It was like playing in the park."

Twenty-nine games unbeaten, Aldridge doing a fine job of replacing Ian Rush, Barnes and Beardsley clicking as if they'd played together forever – the memories go on and on for Hooton.

And he believes the side put together by Dalglish in 1987/88 remains the best Liverpool side he has ever seen.

He said: "The £3m we got for Rush going to Juventus was invested in quality players and that transformed us.

"Although we were great the year before, we saw a different style of football that season.

"We looked unstoppable and they were easily the best team in Europe – and the actual skill involved took us to another level.

"We had seen great sides before that in the 70s and 80s but that season was something completely new and exciting.

"We went to a different level. Barnes was doing things we had never seen before – he could do stuff we had only seen the Brazilians doing. I think they were the best football team I have seen at Liverpool.

"In the end we used to stand on the Kop wishing the opposition would go 2-0 up so we could get a game. We just believed we would win 3-2 – the arrogance that comes with success I suppose. But we were that good we just knew anything was possible."

Hooton has more than one reason to remember 1987/88 as it was also the farewell season of The End – the influential Liverpool fanzine that he set up along with his mates Mick Potter and Phil Jones.

Long before social media and London-based magazines dictated fashion trends, musical tastes and political opinion, The End was blazing the trail on Merseyside. Its first edition in 1981 saw 500 copies printed at a cost of 20p. If every copy sold then they made £10 profit.

Clearly it was never about the money – it was about capturing Liverpool life for Liverpool people attending Liverpool games.

By 1988 Hooton had decided it was becoming too difficult to continue the fanzine despite its fanatical following but looks back fondly on what had become a Kop institution.

"It wasn't a football fanzine as such, it was more about social commentary and satire," he said.

"The reason we stopped The End

in 1988 is because we had stopped going to a lot of away games and we were finding it harder and harder to do.

"We used to go to nearly every away game and sell the magazine on the trains but that was happening less and less – plus the group were getting busier all the time.

"When you get to your mid-20s you also start thinking 'how can we keep writing for a younger audience?' because we were getting older so at the time it seemed like the obvious thing to do was to stop when we got to Issue 20.

"It seemed like a decent round number to stop on.

"Me, Mick and Phil used to go to loads of away games but we decided we should knock it on the head.

"I'm as proud of it today as I was then though – they were amazing times."

ANFIELD RAP

When you think back to how good this Liverpool side was, it's still an astonishing thought, even now, that they didn't go on to complete a league and FA Cup double. The 1-0 defeat to Wimbledon is one of the greatest FA Cup Final shocks of all time, but at least it's not just for the game that Kopites will remember the cup run. Victories over Aston Villa, Everton, Man City and Nottingham Forest were hugely enjoyable – and then came the most famous Liverpool cup final song of all time.

Co-written by Reds winger Craig Johnston and rapper Derek B, The Anfield Rap made it all the way to number three in the UK singles chart. To some Kopites, the tongue-in-cheek rap was so off-the-wall it was brilliant. To others it was excruciatingly bad. Whatever you thought of it, The Anfield Rap lives long in the memory and one or two of you can probably still recite all the words! For those of you who can't, here's how it went and who sung what...

Lyrics	Sung by
Liverpool F.C. is hard as hell United, Tottenham, Arsenal Watch my lips, and I will spell Cos they don't just play but they can rap as well	Barnes
Liverpool F.C. Liverpool F.C.	Grobbelaar
My idea was to build Liverpool into a bastion of invincibility, you know like	Bill Shankly
Liverpool F.C. Liverpool F.C.	Grobbelaar
Napoleon had that idea and he conquered the bloody world	Bill Shankly
Walk on... walk on... with hope... in your heart... and you'll ne...ver walk... alone	Everyone
Alright Aldo? Sound as a pound I'm cushty la but there's nothing down The rest of the lads ain't got it sussed We'll have to learn 'em to talk like us	McMahon Aldridge McMahon Aldridge McMahon/Aldo
Well I'm rapping now, I'm rapping for fun I'm your goalie, the number one You can take the Mick, don't call me a clown Any more lip and you're going down	Grobbelaar
Ar ay ace, we're great me and you But the other lads don't talk like we do No they don't talk like we do, do dey doh la? We'll have to learn 'em to talk propah	McMahon Aldridge McMahon McMahon/Aldo
Walk on... walk on... with hope... in your heart... and you'll ne...ver walk...alone	Everyone
You two Scousers are always yapping I'm gonna show you some serious rapping I come from Jamaica, my name is John Barn-es When I do my thing the crowd go bananas	Barnes
How's he doing the Jamaica rap? He's from just south of the Watford Gap He gives us stick about the north/south divide Cos they got the jobs Yeah but we got the side	Aldridge McMahon Aldridge McMahon McMahon/Aldo
Well I came to England looking for fame So come on Kenny man, give us a game Cos I'm sat on the bench paying my dues and my fees I'm very big down under, but my wife disagrees	Johnston

Lyrics	Sung by
They've won the league, bigger stars than Dallas They got more silver than Buckingham Palace No-one knows quite what to expect When the red machine's in full effect Well Steve McMahon sure can rap It's about time he had an England cap So come on Bobby Robson, he's the man cos if anyone can Macca can... Macca can... Macca can... Macca can... Macca can...	Brian Moore
Liverpool F.C. is hard as hell	Barnes
My idea was to build Liverpool up and up and up Until eventually they would be untouchable Everybody would have to submit Give in, give in, give in	Bill Shankly
We're Highland lads Och-aye the noo And there's four of us And only two of you So if you want nai trouble And you don't want a slap You'd better teach us the Anfield Rap	Nicol Gillespie MacDonald Hansen Nicol Gillespie Nicol/Hansen/ Gillespie/ MacDonald
Don't forget us Paddys And me the Great Dane And I'm from London mate so watch your game Well you two Scousers, you're always squawking But we'll just let our feet do the talking	Beglin/Whelan Molby Spackman Beglin/Whelan/ Spackman/Molby
Our lads have come from all over the place They talk dead funny, but they play dead great Well now we've gotta learn 'em to talk real cool The song you've gotta learn if you live in the Pool	McMahon Aldridge McMahon McMahon/Aldo
Walk on... walk on... with hope... in your heart... and you'll ne... ver walk... alone You'll never walk alone	Everyone
Ho-ho my word, that's unbelievable, it really is I think they should stick to playing football. Terrible What do you think Kenny?	Brian Moore
Oh yeah!	Kenny Dalglish

A FINAL SALUTE

The Wembley finale may not have added the expected gloss to a magnificent season, but it was time to reflect on a remarkable campaign when the Reds played football to an unprecedented standard

TO the victors go the spoils.

Or in this case, to Liverpool go the league championship trophy as well as the Barclays Trophy and a nice little earner of £50,000.

As May opened, Anfield got to salute the men who had entertained them so royally over the previous 10 months. However, once the dust settled on the league celebrations, Liverpool then had to face Southampton and the earlier euphoria fell away as the Reds failed to beat the south coast team in front of 37,610 expectant spectators.

It was not a great way to open the month and it was to end in a similarly disappointing manner in the FA Cup final against Wimbledon.

While that later shock ended Liverpool's seemingly inevitable march towards the league and FA Cup double, there was still time in May for the Reds to once again underline their authority and their brilliance with an emphatic victory over Sheffield Wednesday.

Once again, it was a performance that had it all from a team and a club that had it all.

Over the course of the season the team's quality shone through, as did their sportsmanship.

Before the final home game of the season against Luton, received the PFA Fair Play secretary Gordon Taylor on collecting the least number

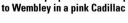

TRAVELLING IN STYLE:
Reds fans prepare for their trip
to Wembley in a pink Cadillac

of disciplinary points over the course of the campaign.

May also saw the return of Jim Beglin to action following his terrible broken leg at Goodison Park the season before. Beglin had spent over 16 months on the sidelines but inched his way back into first XI contention with a series of impressive reserve team performances.

It may have come too late to have an impact on the season but Beglin's comeback gave everyone at Anfield a lift. While Beglin was doing all he could to remain at Anfield, Craig Johnston was doing the opposite – announcing his shock decision to quit England for a return to his native Australia.

That left everybody at the club stunned because Dalglish and everybody else had not seen it coming.

What was a lot more obvious was Dalglish's own personal silverware for pulling off the most entertaining season in living memory.

Although the Reds were disappointed by losing to Wimbledon at Wembley, King Kenny was still comfortably judged the Bells Manager of the Year. The man – who put his immeasurable talents to further use by joining in a charity head shave during May – has always put Liverpool ahead of his own personal ambitions but even he could be proud of the recognition he had received.

A remarkable man. A remarkable manager.

A remarkable season.

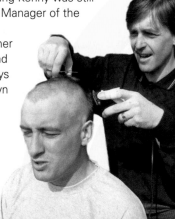

Barclays Football League
Division One
Saturday, May 7
Hillsborough

Sheffield Wednesday 1
Hirst 88

Liverpool 5
*Johnston 31, 90, Barnes 36,
Beardsley 87, 88*

LIVERPOOL'S annihilation of Sheffield Wednesday gave them the chance to emphasise the enormous gulf in class that separates them from most of their rivals.

In his programme comments, Wednesday manager Howard Wilkinson said he felt his squad were now "somewhere near being able to compete with the best."

If that was true then Liverpool must have been playing in a different division.

They were so superior in every aspect that the only real talking point of the afternoon was how they failed to reach double figures.

The Owls' central defence may have been playing largely from memory but the distributive qualities of players like Alan Hansen, Gary Ablett, Steve Nicol, Steve McMahon and Jan Molby were so impressive they even had the home supporters applauding.

In every direction and everywhere Wednesday looked, they were faced by Liverpool players having the time of their lives. Kenny Dalglish's men had produced some astonishing performances during the season and this match was right up there.

Apart from a late consolation for David Hirst, the home side had to sit down and take their medicine.

Craig Johnston scored what felt like an inevitable opener after 31 minutes before also book-ending the scoring with Liverpool's fifth in the last minute. Between those efforts came a John Barnes finish and two from Peter Beardsley.

It had been an almost frighteningly impressive performance.

Sheffield Wednesday: Pressman, Sterland, Worthington, Madden, May, Proctor, West (Galvin), Megson, Chapman, Hirst, Jonsson.
Liverpool: Grobbelaar, Gillespie, Ablett, Nicol, Spackman, Hansen (Molby 46), Beardsley, Aldridge, Houghton, Barnes, McMahon (Whelan 65).

Attendance: 35,893

Uncut fact:
Sheffield Wednesday boss Howard Wilkinson was so impressed with Liverpool's display that he waited at the side of the pitch at full-time to applaud the players off.

Barclays Football League
Division One
Monday, May 2
Anfield

Liverpool 1
Aldridge 41

Southampton 1
R Wallace 67

CORONATION day at Anfield wasn't celebrated with the type of champagne football Liverpool had played during the season, but seeing the Reds parade the championship trophy put Kopites in party mood.

John Aldridge netted his 28th goal of the season shortly before the break before Rod Wallace found an equaliser with just over 20 minutes to go.

Liverpool: Grobbelaar, Gillespie, Ablett, Nicol, Spackman (Whelan 76), Hansen, Beardsley, Aldridge, Houghton, Barnes, McMahon (Johnston 68).
Southampton: Burridge, Forrest, Statham, Case, Moore, Bond, R Wallace, Baker, Clarke, Townsend, D Wallace.

Attendance: 37,610

Uncut fact:
Reds skipper Alan Hansen was presented with the Barclays League trophy before kick-off while the club also received a cheque for £50,000.

Barclays Football League
Division One
Monday, May 9
Anfield

Liverpool 1
Aldridge 17

Luton Town 1
Oldfield 29

LIVERPOOL'S FA Cup final preperations took a knock when Nigel Spackman and Gary Gillespie clashed heads, leaving both needing stitches.

Kevin MacDonald made his first appearance since breaking his leg in September 1986 and John Aldridge scored with an overhead kick, but teenager David Oldfield found an equaliser for the Hatters as the Reds completed their league campaign.

Liverpool: Grobbelaar, Gillespie (MacDonald 75), Ablett, Nicol, Spackman, Whelan, Johnston (Dalglish 75), Aldridge, Houghton, Barnes, McMahon.
Luton: Dibble, Breacker, R Johnson (James), Grimes, Foster, M Johnson, Wilson, Allinson (Cobb), Oldfield, Preece, Black.

Attendance: 30,376

Uncut fact:
The average Anfield attendance for the season was 39,657, which surpassed Manchester United's to make the Reds the best supported Football League club for the first time since 1971/72.

v Southampton

v Luton Town

FA Cup final
Saturday, May 14
Wembley

Liverpool 0

Wimbledon 1
Sanchez

PETER Beardsley had a goal wrongly disallowed and John Aldridge missed a penalty as Wimbledon wrecked Kenny's double-double bid at Wembley.

Lawrie Sanchez's headed goal in the first half proved to be enough to win it for the Crazy Gang.

Liverpool: Grobbelaar, Gillespie, Ablett, Nicol, Spackman (Molby 74), Hansen, Beardsley, Aldridge (Johnston 64), Houghton, Barnes, McMahon (Whelan 65).
Charlton: Beasant, Goodyear, Phelan, Jones, Young, Thorn, Gibson (Scales 64), Cork (Cunningham 58), Fashanu, Sanchez, Wise.

Attendance: 98,203

Uncut fact:
John Aldridge became the first player to miss a penalty at a Wembley FA Cup final when he was denied by a Dave Beasant save.

may 1988

v Wimbledon

FACTS & FIGURES 1987/1988

Kick-off 3 p.m. unless otherwise stated

1987	Fixtures	Res.	1	2	3	4	5	6	7	8	9	10	11	Substitutes	Att.
Aug. 15	Arsenal	2-1	Grobbelaar	Gillespie	Venison	Nicol	Whelan	Hansen	Beardsley	**Aldridge**	Johnston	Barnes	McMahon	**Walsh**/Spackman	54,703
29	Coventry City	4-1	Grobbelaar	Gillespie	Venison	Nicol (2)	Whelan	Hansen	**Beardsley**	**Aldridge**	Johnston	Barnes	McMahon	**Walsh**/Spackman	27,637
Sept. 5	West Ham United	1-1	Grobbelaar	Gillespie	Venison	Nicol	Whelan	Hansen	Beardsley	**Aldridge**	Spackman	Barnes	McMahon	Walsh/Spackman	29,865
12	Oxford United	2-0	Grobbelaar	Gillespie	Venison	Nicol	Whelan	Hansen	Beardsley	**Aldridge**	Spackman	**Barnes**	McMahon	**Walsh**/Wark	42,266
15	Charlton Athletic (7.30 p.m.)	3-2	Grobbelaar	Gillespie	Venison	Nicol	Whelan	**Hansen**	Beardsley	**Aldridge**	Lawrenson	Barnes	**McMahon**	Lawrenson/Walsh	36,637
20	Newcastle United (3.05 p.m.)	4-1	Grobbelaar	Gillespie	Venison	Nicol (3)	Whelan	Hansen	Beardsley	Aldridge	Lawrenson	Barnes	**McMahon**	Spackman/Walsh	24,141
23	Blackburn Rovers L'woods CC(2-1L)(7.30 p.m.)	1-1	Grobbelaar	Spackman	Venison	Nicol	Whelan	Hansen	Beardsley	Aldridge	Lawrenson	Barnes	McMahon	Walsh/Spackman	13,924
29	Derby County (7.30 p.m.)	4-0	Grobbelaar	Gillespie	Venison	Nicol	**Whelan**	Hansen	**Beardsley**	**Aldridge (3)**	Johnston	Barnes	McMahon	**Walsh**/Lawrenson	43,405
Oct. 3	Portsmouth	4-0	Grobbelaar	Gillespie	Venison	Nicol	Whelan	Hansen	Beardsley	**Aldridge**	Johnston	Barnes	**McMahon**	**Walsh**/Lawrenson	44,366
6	Blackburn Rovers L'woods CC(2-2L)(7.30 p.m.)	1-0	Grobbelaar	Gillespie	Venison	Nicol	Whelan	Hansen	Beardsley	**Aldridge**	Johnston	Barnes	McMahon	**Walsh**/Lawrenson	29,994
17	Queen's Park Rangers	4-0	Grobbelaar	Gillespie	Venison	Nicol	Whelan	Hansen	Beardsley	**Aldridge**	**Johnston**	Barnes	Wark	**Walsh**/Lawrenson	43,735
24	Luton Town	1-0	Grobbelaar	Gillespie	Venison	Nicol	Whelan	Hansen	Beardsley	Aldridge	Johnston	**Barnes (2)**	McMahon	Walsh/Lawrenson	12,452
28	Everton L'woods CC(3)(7.30 p.m.)	0-1	Grobbelaar	Gillespie	Venison	Nicol	Whelan	Hansen	Beardsley	Aldridge	Johnston	Barnes	McMahon	Spackman/Walsh	44,071
Nov. 4	Everton (3.05 p.m.)	2-0	Grobbelaar	Gillespie	Lawrenson	Nicol	Whelan	Hansen	Beardsley	Aldridge	Johnston	Barnes	McMahon	Spackman/Walsh	44,260
15	Wimbledon	1-1	Grobbelaar	Gillespie	Lawrenson	Nicol	Whelan	Hansen	Beardsley	Aldridge	Johnston	Barnes	McMahon	Molby/Houghton	13,544
21	Manchester United (2.35 p.m.)	1-1	Grobbelaar	Gillespie	Lawrenson	Nicol	Whelan	Hansen	Beardsley	**Aldridge**	Johnston	Barnes	**McMahon**	**Houghton(1)**/Molby	47,106
24	Norwich City	0-0	Grobbelaar	Gillespie	Lawrenson	Nicol	Whelan	Hansen	Beardsley	Aldridge	Johnston	Barnes	McMahon	Houghton/Spackman	37,446
28	Watford (7.30 p.m.)	4-0	Grobbelaar	Gillespie	Lawrenson	Nicol	Whelan	Hansen	Walsh	**Aldridge**	**Houghton**	Barnes	**McMahon**	Johnston/Spackman	32,396
Dec.	Tottenham Hotspur	2-0	Grobbelaar	Gillespie	Lawrenson	Nicol	Whelan	Hansen	Beardsley	Aldridge	Houghton	Barnes	McMahon	**Walsh**/Spackman	47,362
6	Chelsea (2.35 p.m.)	2-1	Grobbelaar	Gillespie	Lawrenson	Nicol	Whelan	Hansen	Beardsley	**Aldridge**	Houghton	Barnes	**McMahon**	**Johnston(1)**/Spackman	31,211
12	Southampton	2-2	Grobbelaar	Gillespie	Lawrenson	Nicol	Whelan	Hansen	Beardsley	Aldridge	Houghton	Barnes	McMahon	**Johnston**/Spackman	19,507
19	Sheffield Wednesday	1-0	Grobbelaar	**Gillespie**	Lawrenson	Nicol	Whelan	Hansen	Beardsley	Aldridge	Houghton	**Barnes(2)**	McMahon	**Ablett**/Spackman	35,383
26	Oxford United	3-0	Grobbelaar	Gillespie	Venison	Nicol	Whelan	Hansen	Beardsley	**Aldridge**	Houghton	Barnes	McMahon	Johnston/Ablett	13,680
28	Newcastle United	4-0	Grobbelaar	Gillespie	Venison	Nicol	Whelan	Hansen	Beardsley	**Aldridge (2)**	**Houghton**	**Barnes(2)**	**McMahon**	Johnston/Spackman	44,637
1988															
Jan. 1	Coventry City	4-0	Grobbelaar	Gillespie	Venison	Nicol	Whelan	Hansen	**Beardsley (2)**	**Aldridge**	**Houghton**	Barnes	McMahon	**Ablett**/Spackman	38,790
9	Stoke City (FA Cup 3)	0-0	Hooper	Gillespie	Lawrenson	Nicol	Whelan	Hansen	Beardsley	Aldridge	Houghton	Barnes	McMahon	Johnston/Spackman	31,979
12	Stoke City (FA Cup 3 – replay)	1-0	Hooper	Gillespie	Lawrenson	Nicol	Whelan	Hansen	**Beardsley**	Aldridge	Houghton	Barnes	McMahon	**Johnston**/Spackman	39,147
16	Arsenal	2-0	Hooper	Gillespie	Lawrenson	Nicol	Whelan	Hansen	**Beardsley**	**Aldridge**	**Houghton**	**Barnes**	McMahon	Johnston/**Spackman**	44,294
23	Charlton Athletic	2-0	Grobbelaar	Ablett	Venison	Nicol	Spackman	Hansen	**Beardsley**	Aldridge	Houghton	Barnes	McMahon	Johnston/Spackman	28,095
31	Aston Villa (FA Cup 4)(2.35 p.m.)	2-0	Grobbelaar	Ablett	Venison	Nicol	Spackman	Hansen	Beardsley	Aldridge	Houghton	Barnes	McMahon	Johnston/Molby	46,324
Feb. 6	West Ham United	0-0	Grobbelaar	Ablett	Venison	Nicol	Spackman	Hansen	**Beardsley (2)**	Aldridge	Houghton	Barnes	McMahon	**Johnston**/Molby	42,049
13	Watford	4-1	Grobbelaar	Ablett	Venison	Nicol	Spackman	Hansen	Beardsley	**Aldridge**	**Houghton**	**Barnes**	McMahon	Johnston/Dalglish	23,838
21	Everton (FA Cup 5)(3.05 p.m.)	1-0	Grobbelaar	Ablett	Venison	Nicol	Spackman	Hansen	Beardsley	Aldridge	Houghton	Barnes	McMahon	Johnston/Molby	48,270
27	Portsmouth	2-0	Grobbelaar	Ablett	Watson	Nicol	Spackman	Hansen	Beardsley	Aldridge	Houghton	**Barnes**	McMahon	Johnston/Molby	28,171
Mar. 5	Queen's Park Rangers	1-0	Grobbelaar	Gillespie	Ablett	Nicol	Spackman	Hansen	Beardsley	Johnston	Houghton	Barnes	McMahon	Dalglish/Molby	23,171
13	Manchester City (FA Cup-6)(2.35 p.m.)	4-0	Grobbelaar	Gillespie	Ablett	Nicol	Spackman	Hansen	**Beardsley**	Johnston	**Houghton**	**Barnes (2)**	McMahon	Watson/Molby	44,077
16	Derby County (7.30 p.m.)	1-1	Grobbelaar	Gillespie	Ablett	Nicol	Spackman	Hansen	Beardsley	Johnston	Houghton	Barnes	McMahon	MacDonald/Watson	26,356
20	Everton (2.35 p.m.)	0-1	Grobbelaar	Gillespie	Ablett	Nicol	Spackman	Hansen	Beardsley	Aldridge	Houghton	Barnes	McMahon	**Molby**/Watson	44,162
26	Wimbledon	2-1	Grobbelaar	Gillespie	Ablett	Nicol	Spackman	Hansen	Beardsley	**Aldridge**	**Houghton**	**Barnes**	McMahon	**Molby**/Dalglish	36,464
Apr. 2	Nottingham Forest	1-2	Grobbelaar	Gillespie	Ablett	Nicol	Spackman	Hansen	Molby	Aldridge	Johnston	Barnes	McMahon	**Beardsley**/Houghton	29,188
4	Manchester United	3-3	Grobbelaar	Gillespie	Ablett	Nicol	Spackman	Hansen	**Beardsley**	Aldridge	Houghton	**Barnes**	McMahon	**Johnston**/Dalglish	43,497
9	Nottingham Forest (FA Cup SF)(Hillsborough)	2-1	Grobbelaar	**Gillespie**	Ablett	Nicol	Spackman	Hansen	Beardsley	**Aldridge (2)**	**Houghton**	Barnes	McMahon	Molby/Johnston	51,627
13	Nottingham Forest (7.30 p.m.)	5-0	Grobbelaar	Gillespie	Ablett	Nicol	Spackman	Hansen	**Beardsley**	**Aldridge (2)**	Houghton	**Barnes**	McMahon	**Molby**/Johnston	39,535
20	Norwich City (7.30 p.m.)	0-0	Grobbelaar	Gillespie	Ablett	Nicol	Spackman	Hansen	Beardsley	Aldridge	Houghton	Johnston	McMahon	MacDonald/Staunton	22,507
23	Tottenham Hotspur	1-0	Grobbelaar	Gillespie	Ablett	Nicol	Spackman	Hansen	Johnston	Aldridge	Johnston	Johnston	McMahon	Dalglish/MacDonald	44,798
30	Chelsea	1-1	Grobbelaar	Watson	Whelan	Nicol	Spackman	Hansen	Johnston	Aldridge	Houghton	**Barnes**	McMahon	**Beardsley**/Ablett	35,625
May 2	Southampton	1-1	Grobbelaar	Gillespie	Ablett	Nicol	Spackman	Hansen	**Beardsley**	**Aldridge**	Houghton	Barnes	McMahon	**Johnston**/Whelan	37,610
7	Sheffield Wednesday	5-1	Grobbelaar	Gillespie	Ablett	Nicol	Spackman	Whelan	**Beardsley (2)**	**Johnston (2)**	Houghton	Barnes	McMahon	**Molby**/Whelan	35,893
9	Luton Town (7.30 p.m.)	1-1	Grobbelaar	Gillespie	Ablett	Nicol	Spackman	Whelan	Johnston	Johnston (2)	Houghton	Barnes	McMahon	Dalglish/MacDonald	30,376
14	FA Cup final (Wembley)—Wimbledon	0-1	Grobbelaar	Gillespie	Ablett	Nicol	Spackman	Hansen	Beardsley	Aldridge	Houghton	Barnes	McMahon	**Johnston**/Molby	98,203

Home matches in **bold** type   Goalscorers in **bold** type   Substitute in **bold** type when called on

Fixtures copyright Football League Limited and must not be reproduced without permission of Football League Limited

Average home league gate: 39,683
Aggregate home league gate: 793,653

DIVISION 1

1987					F.	A.
Aug.	19—Hull City	a	1	0		
	26—Sheffield United	a	1	2		
Sept.	2—**Huddersfield Town**	h	2	0		
	8—Derby County	a	3	4		
	17—**Manchester City**	h	5	1		
	23—Bradford City	a	2	0		
Oct.	10—**Everton**	h	1	4		
	14—Aston Villa	a	4	0		
	20—**Leicester City**	h	4	0		
	29—Leeds United	a	4	2		
Nov.	7—Everton	a	3	1		
	10—Blackpool	h	6	0		
	17—**Sunderland**	h	5	0		
	28—**Manchester United**	h	2	0		
Dec.	1—Grimsby Town	a	6	0		
	8—**Nottingham Forest**	h	3	1		
	15—Coventry City	a	0	0		
1988						
Jan.	5—**Sheffield Wednesday**	h	1	1		
	19—**Hull City**	h	4	1		
	26—**Derby County**	h	3	0		
Feb.	6—Huddersfield Town	a	1	3		
	11—**Bradford City**	h	6	0		
	16—Manchester City	a	0	2		
	23—**Aston Villa**	h	4	0		
Mar.	7—Leicester City	a	1	2		
	22—Sunderland	a	1	1		
	30—**Blackpool**	h	4	0		
April	4—Manchester United	a	2	0		
	7—**Sheffield United**	h	2	1		
	12—Sheffield Wednesday	a	2	0		
	21—Nottingham Forest	a	0	2		
May	26—**Coventry City**	h	4	1		
	3—**Grimsby Town**	h	3	0		
	18—Leeds United	h	1	2		

Appearances Season 1987-88

Magilton 32, Hooper 31, Durnin 30, Watson 27, Staunton 27, Marsh 27, Boyd 27, MacDonald 21, Jeffers 18, Ablett 17, Molby 16, Wark 14, Walsh 14, Spackman 13, Hayde 12, Johnston 8, Collins 7, Thompson 7, Seagraves 5, De Mange 5, Faccinetti 5, Mooney 4, Fagan 4, Lawrenson 3, Smyth 3, Venison 3, Whelan 3, Hignett 3, Grobbelaar 2, Nesbitt 2, Williams 2, Houghton 1, Beglin 1, Brack 1, Bowman 1, Irvine 1, Dalglish 1, Dures 1, McGorry 1, McVey 1.

Goals

Durnin 23, Walsh 12, Marsh 11, Wark 9, Molby 9, Staunton 8, Jeffers 4, MacDonald 2, Magilton 2, Fagan 2, Ablett 1, Irvine 1, Mooney 1, Thompson 1, Whelan 1

● The Top Twenty records played on this ground are loaned by Robert Crease Music Stores, 14 County Road, Liverpool 4.

Season 1987-88

Team	Pl	W	D	L	F	A	Pts
1 LIVERPOOL	40	26	12	2	87	24	90
2 Manchester Utd	40	23	12	5	71	38	81
3 Nottingham Forest	40	20	13	7	67	39	73
4 Everton	40	19	13	8	53	27	70
5 Q.P.R.	40	19	10	11	48	38	67
6 Arsenal	40	18	12	10	58	39	66
7 Wimbledon	40	14	15	11	58	47	57
8 Newcastle United	40	14	14	12	55	53	56
9 Luton Town	40	14	11	15	57	58	53
10 Coventry City	40	13	14	13	46	53	53
11 Sheffield Wed	40	15	8	17	52	66	53
12 Southampton	40	12	14	14	49	53	50
13 Tottenham	40	12	11	17	38	48	47
14 Norwich City	40	12	9	19	40	52	45
15 Derby County	40	10	13	17	35	45	43
16 West Ham United	40	9	15	16	40	52	42
17 Charlton Athletic	40	9	15	16	38	52	42
18 Chelsea	40	9	15	16	50	68	42
19 Portsmouth	40	7	14	19	36	66	35
20 Watford	40	7	11	22	27	51	32
21 Oxford United	40	6	13	21	44	80	31

CENTRAL LEAGUE

Season 1987-88

Team	Pl	W	D	L	F	A	Pts
1 Nottingham Forest	34	25	2	7	81	37	77
2 LIVERPOOL	34	23	3	8	91	31	72
3 Derby County	34	21	3	10	79	41	66
4 Manchester City	34	20	4	10	74	51	64
5 Sheffield United	34	17	6	11	68	55	57
6 Leeds United	34	15	5	14	58	56	50
7 Sunderland	34	14	8	12	51	54	50
8 Everton	34	14	5	15	57	46	47
9 Sheffield Wed	34	13	8	13	54	52	47
10 Manchester Utd	34	13	8	13	49	48	47
11 Coventry City	34	11	13	10	51	37	46
12 Leicester City	34	14	3	17	61	55	45
13 Huddersfield	34	13	6	15	44	63	45
14 Aston Villa	34	13	5	16	62	69	44
15 Hull City	34	12	6	16	53	61	42
16 Bradford City	34	9	6	19	45	77	33
17 Grimsby Town	34	6	3	25	29	100	21
18 Blackpool	34	3	6	25	23	97	15

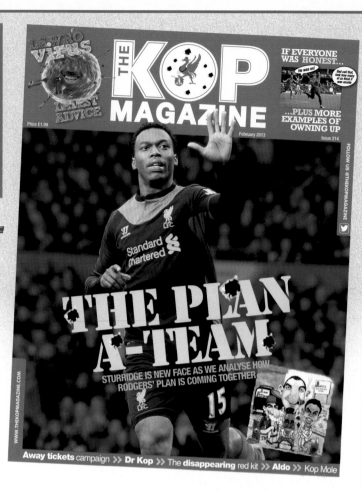

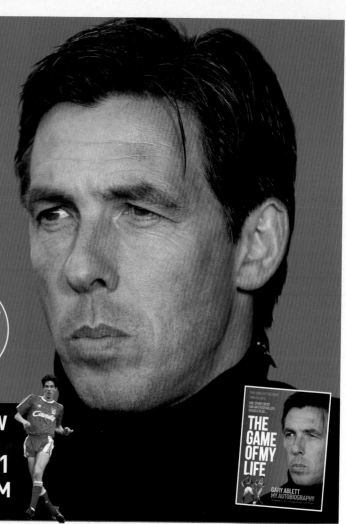